HIGHWAY IN THE SUN

AND OTHER PLAYS

D1452021

Also by Samuel Selvon

SAM SELVON

HIGHWAY IN THE SUN

AND OTHER PLAYS

PEEPAL TREE

First published in Great Britain in 1991
Reprinted in 2008
Peepal Tree Press
17 King's Avenue
Leeds LS6 1QS
England

ISBN 0 948833 07 6
ISBN 13: 9780948833076

Peepal Tree gratefully acknowledges Arts Council support

CONTENTS

HIGHWAY IN THE SUN

Characters

TIGER: A young Indian provisions grower who has just moved to Barataria with his wife.

URMILLA: His young wife, still no more than an adolescent girl.

RITA MARTIN: Tiger's and Urmilla's Afro-Creole neighbour. Rita has a motherly/sisterly concern for Urmilla. She is not frightened to speak her mind to anybody.

JOE MARTIN: Rita's husband, somewhat less enthusiastic about her involvement with their Indian neighbours.

SOOKDEO: An old Indian provisions grower; a drunkard but a literate who teaches Tiger how to read.

TALL BOY: The Chinese shopkeeper in Barataria.

BOYSIE: Tiger's friend, impatient to leave Trinidad for the wider world of the United States.

JOHN: An American supervisor on the road-construction project Tiger works for.

LARRY: Another American supervisor.

DR. WENTWORTH: An English doctor.

INDIAN DOCTOR

CREOLE DOCTOR

POSTMAN

VENDORS, VILLAGERS, CHILDREN

A shop in the village of Barataria, Trinidad, during the war. An old Indian gardener, SOOKDEO, is sitting on a bag of sugar reading the newspapers. RITA MARTIN, an Afro-Trinidadian housewife enters the shop and taps impatiently with a coin on the counter. It is mid-morning.

RITA [*calling*]: Tall Boy... aye... Tall Boy... [*She sucks her teeth as she gets no response, and turns to* SOOKDEO.] Aye, Sookdeo, where this Tall Boy gone at all? Somebody could just walk in the shop and thief something.

SOOKDEO [*vaguely, from behind his newspaper*]: He coming.

RITA [*grumbling*]: He better stop coming and come! I left a pot of peas and rice on the fire... [*Pauses*] I hear you is a teacher now, learning Tiger to read and write?

SOOKDEO [*still behind his paper*]: Mind your own business.

RITA: But Tiger and Urmilla is my neighbours... He have a lot of ambition for his age. Young boy like him just get married... Is how you Indians does get married so young?

SOOKDEO [*angrily*]: You can't see I trying to read in peace, Rita?

RITA: Tiger barely lose his mother features, and as for Urmilla, I doubt she pass fourteen years.

SOOKDEO [*putting his paper down*]: Some people in this Barataria only know to marko other people and find out their business.

RITA [*indignant*]: Listen to this old drunkard! If wasn't for me and Joe – and we is Creoles, mind you – they see hell to settle down in that old carat hut.

SOOKDEO: Just because your house make of concrete and you have electric light, you don't have to get on so.

RITA [*snorting*]: Ahh... Why you don't go and work in your garden... [TALL BOY, *the young Chinese proprietor, appears.*] ... Tall Boy, listen to this old bend-up piece of wire... I was the first one to make friends when they come to Barataria to live.

TALL BOY: What you want, Rita?

RITA: You promise to keep some fresh hops bread for me.

TALL BOY: You come too late.

RITA: But you promise, man!

TALL BOY: You forget it have a war on? You forget everything ration now? People fighting in the bakery in town to get a loaf of bread, and you strolling in here mid-morning...

RITA [*interrupting*]: I don't want to hear no nonsense 'bout no war!

9

It ain't have no war in Trinidad. You promise me two hops bread and I left the money with you.

TALL BOY: In all the rush this morning, I really forget... you want your money back? ...I tell you what [*He lowers his voice.*] I getting some smoke herring tomorrow.

RITA: In truth?

TALL BOY: Yes. A shipment come, and I done arrange things in town. But you better come early, Rita, you know it like an invasion when people find out.

RITA: I won't tell nobody... Keep some for me, eh. And Urmilla.

TALL BOY: I got to share fair... Urmilla have to come for she own.

RITA: All right... I suppose I better take two pound of flour and make johny-cake.

TALL BOY: Two pound! For you and who? You know is one pound for each customer.

RITA: Man Tall Boy, I got to feed that hefty husband of mine. When Joe sit down to eat is trouble... Bring two pound and stop making joke.

TALL BOY [*reluctant*]: Only as it's you.

RITA [*as he moves to get it*]: And a pound of split peas same time.

TALL BOY: You know split peas gone up? Is a shilling a pound now.

RITA: Lord, everything going up, nothing coming down. I better start up a garden like Tiger and them other Indians in the village...

SOOKDEO: It need some skill for that...

RITA [*scornful*]: Like you. Sitting on your tail in the shop all day, waiting for a free rum.

SOOKDEO: But when croptime come, old Sookdeo reaping the most! [*Chuckles to himself*]

TALL BOY: Anything else?

RITA: Am... Oh yes. Urmilla say to send half-pound saltfish, and to mark it.

TALL BOY: I ain't marking nothing! Tiger still owe me five dollars from last week.

RITA [*wheedling*]: Go on, you know you going to give me...

TALL BOY: All right. But tell Urmilla... all that milk she selling from the cow must be bringing in some money

RITA: Give them a chance. Tiger going to pick tomatoes next week, and he go pay you.

SOOKDEO [*with sarcastic amazement*]: But eh-eh! This woman is a real marko!... Is which side of the bed Tiger does sleep on?

RITA: They ain't have no bed. They sleep on the floor... and that poor girl pregnant.

SOOKDEO [*egging her on*]: Go on, Rita, go on!

RITA: And to tell you... [*She stops, realising the old man is making fun of her. He and* TALL BOY *burst out laughing: she is furious.*] ... You old drunkard! No wonder the children always teasing you... and I hear you was drunk last night and rolling in the canal on the main road near Jumbie Bridge...

[TIGER *enters the shop. He has been working in his garden.* RITA *wheels as she sees him.*]

RITA: Ah, Tiger!

TIGER: What's the argument about?

RITA: Look at you with cutlass and hoe! You're a worker, not like this old vagabond... I sure his garden must be full of rabbit-grass and mary-shut-your-gate!

TIGER [*resting his hoe and cutlass on the counter*]: It ain't. No weeds at all. Is the cleanest garden in the whole village.

SOOKDEO: Tell she, Tiger, tell she!

RITA: Must be obeah then, cause he don't do no work... Come, Tall Boy, give me my message, let me go... and mark it till Joe get pay on Friday.

TIGER: Have a drink with me, Rita?

RITA: I don't drink rum in this hot sun! You better don't let that old scamp encourage you... and all this thing about learning education...

SOOKDEO [*teasing*]: You want me read the papers and tell you the war news?

RITA [*ready to go*]: I don't want to know about no evil war in England and Germany. We have enough worries in little Trinidad... [*She stalks out of the shop.*]

SOOKDEO: You late, Tiger.

TIGER: I was hoeing that patch in the right hand at the back, near the swamp.

SOOKDEO: I was thirsty, but Tall Boy wouldn't trust me.

TIGER [*slowly, as if testing his words*]: I told you, that in future negotiations, you are to let Mr. Sookdeo have what he wants...

11

[*In a natural voice now*] How you like that?

SOOKDEO [*in an emotional voice*]: Let me get off this sugar bag… Say that again, Tiger, say it again!

TIGER: What?

SOOKDEO: What you call me! The *Mister* part!

TIGER: Well, you yourself tell me is a term of respect. And I respect you.

SOOKDEO: You witness, Tall Boy? Nobody in this village ever call me *Mister* before… This boy going to go a long way… Bring the drinks, and mark it on my account.

TALL BOY: Your account! Since when you have account here?

TIGER: Mark it on mine, Tall Boy, and done the talk.

SOOKDEO: No! Open one up for me. And don't forget the *Mister*.

TALL BOY [*doubtful*]: You serious?

SOOKDEO: Yes.

TALL BOY: You have any guarantee?

SOOKDEO: I still alive, ain't I?

TALL BOY: I prefer house and land.

TIGER [*impatient*]: Go on, bring the drinks. I just come out of the hot sun working, and I thirsty.

SOOKDEO: Familiarity breeds contempt! Tiger, write that in your note book. Observe this Chinese foreigner asking me for security! A man like me, born and bred in Trinidad.

TALL BOY [*plonking bottle and glasses on the counter*]: You lucky Tiger buying, is what I say.

SOOKDEO: I have money! Unbeknownst to this village… mark the word, Tiger… *unbeknownst*…

TIGER [*pouring drink*]: Okay… fire one…

TALL BOY: I might as well have one with you-all…

TIGER: Cheers… [*They drink.*]

SOOKDEO [*with a loud sigh*]: Ah… that went down nice…

TIGER: What the papers have today? Any good news?

SOOKDEO: Yes. The Germans winning.

TALL BOY: That is good news?

SOOKDEO: It good for *somebody*! … I could have another, Tiger?

TIGER: Sure, don't ask… You know, I got a feeling something going to happen.

TALL BOY: Like what so?

TIGER: I don't rightly know… Just a feeling.

12

TALL BOY: Rain going to fall?

TIGER: Not that kind of feeling...

SOOKDEO: The word is *premonition*. Write it down else you forget.

TALL BOY: Whatever it is, what you expect to happen in this half-dead village? One day just like another. Is only in England and America big things does happen.

SOOKDEO: You shouldn't cry down you own country like that. All that money what you making off Trinidadians and sending to China...

TALL BOY: Nobody don't bother with this little island.

TIGER: You forget we have oil? Every week ships from all over the world does come here for oil.

SOOKDEO: And what about the Americans? They putting up bases all over the Caribbean...

TALL BOY: Ah, but that ain't have nothing to do with we here in Barataria! What *I* feel is that things would change if the Germans drop a bomb on we...

TIGER: Boysie say he see Yankee troops marching in Port of Spain last week...

TALL BOY: What I mean is, everybody going about their business as usual, though saltfish and rice ration... You take it from me, the war would finish and we wouldn't even know it had one...

[*There is the sound of a bicycle bell ringing in the distance...*]

SOOKDEO: You hear the postman coming?

TIGER: He late today...

TALL BOY: I wonder if he have anything for me?

SOOKDEO: Like a receipt from China for all that money you been sending?

TIGER: Look, he stopping here, anyway. Must be thirsty.

TALL BOY [*raising his voice*]: Aye, don't bring your bicycle in the shop.

POSTMAN [*remaining near the door*]: Take this notice from me, Tiger. I late already.

TIGER [*going to him*]: What notice?

POSTMAN: This... [*Raises his voice*]... Tall Boy, the estate office say you must stick it up in your shop for everybody to see... Put a bottle of beer on the ice for me, when I passing back. [*He goes.*]

SOOKDEO: Here, let me see what it is, Tiger.

TALL BOY: I hope is no advertisement thing, otherwise I charge them.

13

TIGER [*pause*]: Well, what it say?

SOOKDEO [*as if reading to himself*]: … agreement with the Government… proposed highway to run through estate property in Barataria… [*Gets wildly excited*] Oh Lord! Big thing happening! You was feeling right, Tiger!

TIGER: What is it then?

SOOKDEO: Pour a drink for me! Everything finish! The Yankees going to build a road through we land!

TIGER: You lie! Let me see! [*He snatches the paper from* SOOKDEO *and reads.*]

SOOKDEO: It even have a map how the road going and go!

TIGER: [*impatiently*] Don't get so excited, man. Wait, let me see… What's this? C-o-m-p…

SOOKDEO: Compensation!

TIGER: What it mean?

TALL BOY: Money.

SOOKDEO: Yes, they going to pay we for the land. But…

[*There are a few moments of stunned silence…*]

TIGER: Sudden so, out of the blue? You didn't see anything in the papers, Sookdeo?

SOOKDEO: No.

TIGER [*disbelieving*]: But how could they do a thing like that to we? This is a hell of a thing, man. What going to happen to all the people in the village?

SOOKDEO: I ain't selling my land to no Americans.

TIGER: Me neither.

TALL BOY: All-you forget in wartime it does have emergencies. Look how the Yankees already take land to make base. The Government could do anything when is war.

SOOKDEO: Tiger, you best hads go to the estate office in San Juan and find out what all this is about. You know the place?

TIGER: Yes… Watch my hoe and cutlass for me… And you better stick up the notice, Tall Boy, for everybody to see…

It is later in the morning. RITA *is scrubbing clothes over a tub in her yard, humming a tune as she works…* URMILLA *comes in carrying a pail from her milk round. She is shy and soft-spoken…*

RITA [*raised voice*]: Aye, Urmilla, you come back?

14

URMILLA [*approaching the fence to talk*]: Yes Rita. I sell every drop of milk... Whew! It hot for so, eh?

RITA: Come under the mango tree... [*She washes intermittently as she talks to* URMILLA.] ... How you feeling?

URMILLA: So-so.

RITA: All now you should be resting and eating good food to keep up your strength, instead of walking about in the hot sun.

URMILLA: I have plenty things to do... Aye, Rita, I feel it moving last night!

RITA: Yes?

URMILLA: Right here... I wake up Tiger, but when he put his hand he say he ain't feeling nothing. But it was moving. Like he was kicking.

RITA: How you know is a *he*?

URMILLA: Tiger want a boy-child.

RITA: He got to take what he get.

URMILLA: I only praying and hoping is a boy. He keeping after me all the time, warning me that it best hads be a boy... We can't do anything to make sure?

RITA: Only the good lord decide that. Tiger playing so much smart-brains learning to read and write, and he don't know a simple thing like that? It ain't have no invention could help.

URMILLA: What about *vet-e-veh* and *zig-a-lee* bush?

RITA [*snorting*]: Ha, don't bother with bush medicine, I know a woman what dead trying out them thing. She belly swell up big and bust... But why it is you Indians does only want boy-child?

URMILLA: I won't mind if is a girl... is only Tiger... [*She sighs.*] On top of that, all these books and papers he reading... He not like long time, you know. Is only big words now what I can't understand.

RITA: He playing big man, that's all. But he got to creep before he walk... When the baby born it go change him back.

URMILLA: I hope so...

RITA [*lifting a shirt from the tub*]: Look at this shirt collar. How Joe expect me to clean that?

URMILLA: I better get on with my washing, as you say that.

RITA: Bring it.

URMILLA: No man Rita, you have enough to do.

RITA: Go on, my hands in the tub already... Is not too much?

15

URMILLA: Only two shirt and a khaki pants… You sure, Rita? I really feel a little dizzy in the hot sun.

RITA: In your condition you shouldn't be doing nothing.

URMILLA: I feel all right, with you to look after me and deliver the baby… I don't know what we would of done if wasn't for you, Rita. You been so good to we since we come here to live.

RITA [*gruffly, to hide emotion*]: Don't try to sweeten me up… Look, you want this trousers? Tiger could wear it to work in the garden.

URMILLA: Joe don't want it?

RITA: Joe have plenty… Go on, take it! You could hang it to dry on the fence… and bring the dirty clothes before I change my mind…

Later that evening, in TALL BOY's *shop. Most of the* VILLAGERS *are there to discuss the threatened loss of their land for the road. There is a hubbub of voices and much drinking…*

TIGER [*loudly, above the din*]: All right, all right! Everybody don't talk at one time.

VILLAGER [*as the din lessens*]: We don't want to hear you, Tiger! You just a force-ripe man! [*General laughter*]

TIGER [*angrily*]: I take time off my work to go and find out, though! And ask you-all to come here this evening… [*Patiently*] Boysie, keep quiet a little…

BOYSIE [*a little older than* TIGER]: I ain't keeping quiet, though all I interested in is the compensation part. I have ochro, tomatoes, and watercress growing… How much you think I would get in hard cash?

TIGER: You not the only one with crops.

VILLAGER: And why they should curry-favour Sookdeo, the old bow-legged scamp?

TIGER: Is because his plot of land right down at the end, and the road not going to pass there.

BOYSIE: Oho! That's why he just sit down there drinking free rum and ain't saying a word!

SOOKDEO: You better learn to respect your elders, Boysie.

TIGER: We got to treat this thing serious. What going to happen when the Americans come? No more land to work on. What you-all going to do? You can't live off compensation money for ever.

16

BOYSIE: Every man got to work out his own business. Is no sense just talking. I for one going and get a work with the Yankees on that road, and save up my money. And then bam! I off for the States, leaving all of you in little Trinidad!

VILLAGER: Boysie right! Is every man for himself.

BOYSIE: Maybe Tiger frighten about what going to happen to him, and trying to get all of we frighten too.

TIGER: I not frighten. I only thinking.

BOYSIE: Come and have a drink and stop thinking. You know what thought make a man do? Tall Boy! What happen to all that ice?

TALL BOY: You-all drinking ice or rum?

BOYSIE: You should get a *frigideer*. What you going to do when them Yankees come in thirsty for rum and coca-cola?

TALL BOY: That's true... I think I got to get another ice box. And stock up with a lot of drinks...

TIGER: How much is a Yankee dollar, Boysie?

BOYSIE: One worth about two Trinidad ones.

TIGER: So much?

BOYSIE: Yes... that's why, boy, I going America to live. What chance a man have here? You get a piece of land and grow some yam, and that's your whole life.

TIGER: It have other things too.

BOYSIE: What other things?

TIGER: Well, you married and have a family... you save up money and educate you children so they won't be stupid as you...

BOYSIE: You talking like an old man. My father and mother did after me to married too, but I run from that... This garden work only part-time with me. In the evening I help my brother drive taxi... If you don't watch out, you come like old Sookdeo!... Sookdeo, you ever been to town?

SOOKDEO: What for?

BOYSIE: You see what I mean? Port of Spain only five miles away, and Sookdeo would dead and he never set foot out of this village. He wife dead, he children left him, and he only have rum to keep him company in old age.

TIGER: Leave him alone, Boysie. You going to get old one day, too.

BOYSIE: But before that happen I want to do things... and I won't end up like him, I could tell you... Pass the bottle.

TIGER: Too much drinking going on here tonight, I want to keep a clear head… It look to me like everybody getting excited and they don't know what going to happen to them.

BOYSIE: That's your feeling, not mine! You know how much money them fellars making who working with the Yanks in the bases? Boy, this is the best thing that could happen to me.

SOOKDEO: But money ain't everything, you know.

BOYSIE [*sneering*]: That's why you bumming drinks… You want another one?

TIGER: Look, I buying a rounds and then I pulling out. I want to go and see Joe.

BOYSIE: He would tell you about working for the Yanks… Ain't he got a job in the base?

TIGER: Yes… Tall Boy, I paying next rounds.

BOYSIE: One for the road?

TIGER: No.

TALL BOY: Push in the doors for me as you going, Tiger… is pass eight o'clock…

TIGER [*leaving*]: Okay.

TIGER *leaves. A little later he approaches* JOE's *house.* JOE *is sitting in the gallery…*

JOE: You back early, man.

TIGER: Yes… How you did know about the meeting?

JOE: Rita tell me… What you-all decide?

TIGER: Every man for himself.

JOE: Sit down… The gallery is the coolest place in the house… Rita over there keeping Urmilla company.

TIGER [*sitting in a bamboo chair*]: It wasn't no meeting in truth. Just a lot of talk and rum flowing like water.

JOE: Well, it should have a lot of work going with the Americans.

TIGER: That's what I wanted to ask you… Boysie say one Yankee dollar worth two of we own, true?

JOE: I never work it out, but something like that… You intend to take a work with them?

TIGER: I suppose I have to in the end… I feel this is a big thing, but nobody as if they care, as long as they have some food to eat, rum to drink, and a place to sleep.

JOE [*cool*]: Don't worry, just see about yourself.

TIGER: That's exactly what I doing. I have ambition, boy. My father

18

uses to mark a big X when they ask him to sign his name. I never forget that, Joe.

JOE: A lot of people can't read nor write.

TIGER: And don't even know we fighting a war! I don't want to grow up stupid...

[*He is interrupted by a shout from* RITA *next door...*]

RITA: Tiger! You over there?

TIGER: Yes!

RITA: Come quick and feel the baby moving!

JOE [*shouting*]: *You* better come home and stop playing midwife.

TIGER [*excited*]: See you later, Joe... [*He runs off.*]

RITA [*from over the fence*]: You should shame encouraging Tiger in idle talk when his wife ain't seen him since six o'clock this morning.

JOE [*disgusted*]: Ah-h-h... I can't get a feel too?

In TIGER'*s and* URMILLA'*s hut...*

TIGER [*a little breathless*]: He really moving?

URMILLA: Yes, Tiger. Come put your hand here... You feel it?

TIGER: Yes... He kicking strong!

RITA [*sternly*]: You still with this *he* business? You think Urmilla is a machine?

TIGER: I done already warn she...and I want him born in full moon.

RITA [*laughs ironically*]: You also saying *when*? But you bold-face with yourself.

URMILLA [*anxiously*]: When is full moon, Rita?

RITA [*thoughtful*]: I think is this week... *That* part might come true.

URMILLA [*apprehensive*]: So quick?

RITA: Might be any day now... That's why you must rest. And don't worry, I will help you when your time come... I better go before that husband of mine start to get on.

URMILLA: Thanks, Rita... Good night...

[RITA *goes.*]

What happen in the shop?

TIGER: Ah, these people in Barataria too foolish. I just waste my time with that meeting. I should of known.

URMILLA: But what we going to do if the garden go?

19

TIGER: Don't aggravate me with no questions. Go and bring some dinner for me... You buy pitch-oil for the lamp?

URMILLA: Yes, Tiger. And I put your books right there in the corner... I wash your dirty pants today...

TIGER: Good thing... this trousers have mud on it... Go and prepare my banquet.

URMILLA: Ban... quet?

TIGER [*impatient*]: The food, woman! The bhagi and roti, or maybe you cook something different for a change?

URMILLA: You like bhagi...

TIGER [*disgustedly*]: It ain't even an *English* word... Just bring the food, hot or cold, I got enough on my brains than try to educate you...

Two nights later in TIGER*'s and* URMILLA*'s hut. There is a high wind soughing the trees. They sleep on the floor.* URMILLA *is restless, feeling pains. She moans a little, hoping to waken* TIGER. *But he sleeps on. Her pain increases. She shakes him...*

URMILLA: Tiger!... Wake up... [*Louder*] Tiger!

TIGER [*startled from deep sleep*]: Eh? What... Oh...

URMILLA: I don't feel too good, you best hads call Rita.

TIGER: What o'clock is it?

URMILLA: I don't know.

TIGER [*yawning*]: The wind is high... listen... I hope it don't blow down the bigan trees in the garden...

URMILLA [*urgently*]: Tiger, I not feeling well. *Get Rita!*

TIGER: Is full moon tonight?

URMILLA [*gasping*]: I don't know... Get Rita, *please*...

TIGER [*gets up*]: If is not full moon, best try and keep him a little longer....

URMILLA: I can't, Tiger... Oh! [*Lapses into groans of pain*]

TIGER [*dressing hurriedly*]: All right... wait a little... just let me get my pants on...

URMILLA: Hurry up...

[TIGER *goes out and crosses to* JOE*'s and* RITA*'s. He knocks on the glass window softly, then louder...*]

TIGER [*in an urgent low tone*]: Rita!... Rita!

RITA [*the window opens. Rita answers sleepily*]: Tiger?

TIGER: The thing happening, come quick!

RITA [*wide awake now*]: Why you didn't call me before? Go and light the fire and hot some water.

TIGER: Yes Rita... anything else?

RITA: Just keep out of the way... You better stay over here with Joe.

[RITA *goes out to tend* URMILLA. JOE *comes out of the house, sleepily and irritably to keep* TIGER *company...*]

JOE [*grumbling*]: I got to work tomorrow, you know.

TIGER: I can't wait alone, man... I must have somebody to talk to.

JOE: Friendship is one thing, but waking a man up like this...

TIGER [*anxious*]: Suppose something happen to Urmilla? Rita know what she is doing?

JOE [*sarcastic*]: A bit late to ask that, ain't you? But don't worry. She deliver plenty babies around here... always poking she nose in other people business.

TIGER: How come you never had a child, Joe?

JOE [*half-grunt, half-laugh*]: You mean with Rita! [*Vaguely*] Maybe after the war, when things settle down... The moon bright, eh?

TIGER: Yes. Is a good sign.

JOE [*facetious*]: The pundit read the stars, eh? Old Sookdeo read your fortune?

TIGER: He ain't no pundit.

JOE: I thought all of them old Indian fellars was pundits... living on the banks of the Ganges, though they in Trinidad!

TIGER: All right for you to make joke, but I got a wife who bringing a baby this minute.

JOE [*yawning*]: That's your funeral... You make yourself at home, because I going back to sleep...

RITA [*shouting from the fence*]: Tiger!

TIGER [*to* JOE]: Like something happen... [*He goes quickly to the fence.*] What happen, Rita?

RITA [*distressed*]: You better get a doctor, it getting complicated.

TIGER: A doctor! This hour? Is almost midnight!

RITA [*snappishly*]: Don't argue with me! Go get Boysie to take you in the taxi... Hurry up!

TIGER [*hesitating*]: Urmilla...

RITA: Don't waste time!

TIGER: All right, all right...

[*He dashes off.* JOE *comes to* RITA.]

JOE: What happen?

RITA [*calmer*]: I just send Tiger for the doctor to make sure…

JOE [*in drawling reproach*]: Same damn thing I thought would happen one day. You shouldn't interfere.

RITA: You better run the extension cord; let we have some light over here.

JOE: Why you don't wash your hands of the whole thing?

RITA [*patiently*]: Go and bring the cord. And a bulb.

JOE [*moving off, grumbling*]: I don't even know which part it is. Must be in the garret…

TIGER *and* BOYSIE *are standing in a street looking for the* DOCTOR's *house…*

BOYSIE: …That house there, across the road.

TIGER [*hesitant*]: It ain't have no light…

BOYSIE: Go and knock, man. Is a Indian doctor live there…

[TIGER *knocks hesitantly at the door. There is no reply…*]

BOYSIE [*impatient*]: Knock hard, man!

[TIGER *knocks louder. Finally a window is opened and the irritated* DOCTOR *looks down on* TIGER.]

INDIAN DOCTOR [*angrily*]: Who is that?

TIGER [*insecure*]: Is… is me, Tiger! My wife sick!

INDIAN DOCTOR: Tiger? Who Tiger?

TIGER: She making baby…

INDIAN DOCTOR: Look man, why you don't take her to the hospital?

TIGER: Hospital?

INDIAN DOCTOR [*testily*]: Yes, yes. That's the best thing. I can't help you…

TIGER: But…

[*The window slams shut…* TIGER *walks slowly back to* BOYSIE *across the street…*]

TIGER: But this is a hell of a thing, Boysie!

BOYSIE: Come let we go, man. You don't know these people what have money, boy, they don't care if anybody else live or dead.

TIGER: But the man is Indian like myself!

22

BOYSIE: Come, we try a Creole doctor just down the road…

[*They go out. A little later they stop in front of a house from which music and the sounds of a party come.*]

TIGER: What this doctor name?

BOYSIE: I can't remember… but he living here.

TIGER [*put off by the party sounds*]: You think he go come?

BOYSIE: Man, go and try! How will you know unless you ask?

[TIGER *goes up to the door and knocks loudly and waits. Soon after the* DOCTOR *opens the door.*]

CREOLE DOCTOR [*abruptly*]: What you want?

TIGER: You is the doctor?

CREOLE DOCTOR: Yes.

TIGER: My wife sick too bad. She making a baby… You could come? Look I have a taxi waiting…

CREOLE DOCTOR: You try that Indian doctor up the road?

TIGER: I just come from there. He slam the window in my face.

CREOLE DOCTOR [*impatient*]: Well look man, I have guests… I can't leave them. Get a midwife. It have one in San Juan.

TIGER [*growing more desperate*]: The neighbour who looking after she say it complicated…

CREOLE DOCTOR: You people so blooming ignorant! You don't know it have a hospital for that sort of thing? You does keep fowl?

TIGER [*puzzled*]: Keep fowl?

CREOLE DOCTOR: How you going to pay me? If you had some chickens…

TIGER: I go get money from somewhere…

CREOLE DOCTOR: Ah, look man, take your wife to the hospital… Or else ask the taxi driver take you to town, by Dr. Wentworth, round by the savannah. He is a white man always playing good Samaritan…

[*The* DOCTOR *shuts the door. This second rebuff leaves* TIGER *stunned. He walks back to* BOYSIE *in a confused state of mind.*]

BOYSIE: What happen? He coming or he coming?

TIGER: Eh?

BOYSIE: Wake up man like you dreaming!

TIGER: He ain't coming… You know one Dr. Wentworth in town? By the savannah?

BOYSIE: We could ask somebody. Come let we go quick… [*They start walking away,* TIGER *dragging behind.*]

BOYSIE: What you studying? Nothing won't happen to Urmilla.

TIGER: Is not that.

BOYSIE: What then?

TIGER [*slowly*]: Nothing…

BOYSIE: Well choo me if you don't want to talk… Let we go quick… [*They leave.*]

Back at JOE's *and* RITA's, *she is dismantling a small bed…*

JOE: What you doing now?

RITA: Don't ask stupid questions, can't you see? Help me take this bed over. You expect doctor to visit and see that poor girl on the floor?

JOE: What the hell happening here tonight? First you playing midwife. Next you wasting electric current. Now you giving them a bed too!

RITA: Take hold of that end down there and lift…

JOE [*warming for an argument*]: And another thing I notice, *madam*… Is which part Tiger get that stripe shirt he wearing? And what happen to my old khaki pants?

RITA: Stop arguing and lift the bed, man… The people is your next door neighbours.

JOE: You always interfering, interfering…

RITA: Look, I taking over the mattriss… You bring along the rest. I can't leave Urmilla alone for long.

JOE [*sarcastic*]: What about a pillow? And some clean sheets?

RITA [*moving off*]: I come back for that after.

JOE [*muttering angrily to himself*]: Sarcasm lost on this woman… I better keep quiet before she give way the whole house…

URMILLA's *hut.* RITA *enters putting down the mattress.*

RITA: There! Joe bringing the rest.

URMILLA [*weakly*]: Why you bothering to take so much trouble, Rita?

RITA [*gruffly*]: You keep quiet… I don't know how Tiger expect you to be on the floor like that…

URMILLA: You too good, Rita. You too good.

RITA [*gently*]: How you feeling now? You want me sap your head with some more bayrum?

URMILLA: Don't worry… You sit down and rest a little, you been on your feet all the time…

JOE [*entering with the rest of the bed*]: Where you putting this?

RITA: Just here… it ain't have no place else! Help me mount it up.

URMILLA [*as they fix the bed*]: Joe, you-all bothering so much… You must be tired yourself and want to sleep…

JOE: Ah. Is no trouble, Urmilla… Don't fret.

RITA: I better keep hot water going on the fire… Just finish put up the bed, Joe.

URMILLA: I not feeling so bad now, I could help…

RITA: You stay just where you is! See she don't budge an inch, Joe, while I in the back. [*She goes out.*]

JOE: I better put a brighter bulb in the cord.

URMILLA: That good enough, Joe… I never see the hut with so much light in it…

JOE: Wait! As if I hear a car coming… [*Sounds of a car approaching on a bumpy road*] Yes… Must be them. I better get Rita…

[*The car stops. Doors open and slam shut. Then* TIGER *and the* ENGLISH DOCTOR *enter the hut.*]

TIGER [*anxiously*]: You all right, Urmilla?

URMILLA: Yes… Rita been looking after me…

TIGER [*noticing the bed for the first time*]: Oh… where the bed come from?

RITA: Ask questions later, Tiger. Give the doctor a chance…

DR. WENTWORTH: Yes… Let me have a look at her…

RITA [*in a low voice to* TIGER]: You and Joe better go over, out of the way. I'll call if we need you…

A little later… TIGER *and* JOE *are sitting on the back steps drinking.* TIGER *breathes out deeply. He is still pensive, pondering his experiences…*

TIGER: Thanks, Joe. I needed that one.

JOE: I thought you-all had a breakdown, you stay so long.

TIGER: Boy, I had a hell of an experience tonight. I never thought big doctors and them so small-minded.

JOE: What happen?

25

TIGER: You know that Indian doctor up by the main road? The man
    slam the window when I tell him my wife was sick… A Indian
    like myself, Joe!… Then we went by a Creole one in San Juan.
    He want to know if I does keep fowl, and turn his back on me.
    My wife could of dead and they won't care, just because I poor…
    You see why I don't want to grow up ignorant, Joe?
JOE [*agreeing*]: Some of them like that.
TIGER: What hurt me most is that this white doctor didn't even ask
    me if I could pay… Your own countrymen would let you down,
    and a man what don't even belong to Trinidad come to my old
    carat hut… I won't forget that for a long time, Joe.
JOE: That's the way life is… If you had my experiences, you just try
    and live happy by yourself. Because you can't change it…
TIGER [*after a long pause*]: You know what I would like to do?
JOE: What?
TIGER: It hard to explain… but I want to be a real man, Joe, to think
    for myself, and make decisions… I bet you don't know why the
    sky blue?
JOE: It blue because it blue, that's all.
TIGER: But why, Joe, why? Why it ain't red or yellow instead? And
    things like what I is… why I born… what I doing here… what
    all of we doing in the world… You know what I mean?
JOE: You best hads don't play scholar and get mad like Spit-in-the-
    Sea!
TIGER: Who is that?
JOE: A old Indian fellar in town… uses to study the Bible day and
    night, and read some high books. All of a sudden, every morning
    precisely at eight o'clock the man going down by the wharf and
    spitting in the sea.
TIGER: Why?
JOE: Ha, that's it! Why? He must of thought he making the sea
    bigger!
RITA [*coming out of the hut, shouting excitedly*]: Tiger! Come!
TIGER [*jumping up, startled*]: Jeez, Joe! We sit down here and forget
    all about the baby!… [*Shouts*] Coming Rita!

In TIGER's *and* URMILLA's *hut, faint cries of a baby.* TIGER *dashes in…*

TIGER: It born, Rita, it born?
RITA: Yes… here, you want to hold it?

26

TIGER [*nervously*]: No… not yet. Is a boy-child?

DR. WENTWORTH: It's a girl. A good eight pounds, too, I'd guess.

TIGER [*disappointed*]: They didn't tell you I wanted a boy?

DR. WENTWORTH [*small laugh*]: They don't come to order… Is the taxi there?

TIGER: Yes sir.

DR. WENTWORTH: Well, I'll be getting along… Let your wife take it easy for a few days.

TIGER: What about… How much we owe you?

RITA: Joe and me will fix that up, Tiger… We could settle up later, when you get your compensation.

DR. WENTWORTH: I'll be sending you a bill… You don't have to pay it all at once… Good night.

TIGER: Good night, doctor… Boysie waiting to take you back…

[*The* DOCTOR *leaves.* TIGER *is upset by everything that evening and gives vent to his feelings…*]

TIGER: I didn't want no girl!

URMILLA [*weakly*]: Next time I will make a boy please God…

TIGER: I getting let down left right and centre tonight.

RITA: You should praise the Lord for small mercies… Look Tiger, now ain't no time to quarrel. Urmilla had a hard time, and she should be sleeping. I going and left the bed with you for a few days till she better, and you come to your proper senses…

A week later in the village market. There are VENDORS *hawking, dogs barking,* CHILDREN *teasing* SOOKDEO, URMILLA *selling milk…*

VENDOR ONE [*in a sing-song voice*]: Any emp-ty bo-ttles?

VENDOR TWO: Fish! Get your fish! Cavalee, kingfish, moonshine…

URMILLA: Milk! Fresh cow's milk!

VENDOR THREE: Man-go! Man-go passing! Mango starch, mango do-doos…

CHILDREN: Sookdeo Sookdeo your pants are all tear Sookdeo Sookdeo you want a kick there…

SOOKDEO [*angrily*]: Let me catch one of you with this stick!

URMILLA: Milk! Get your milk!

TALL BOY [*coming out of his shop*]: Aye Urmilla! You passing straight?

URMILLA: Lord, Tall Boy, sun was so hot I nearly forgot you. And I was thinking.

27

TALL BOY: You catch that disease from Tiger? Just because you had a child. When I get a wife you going to see little Tall Boys and Tall Girls running all over the shop.

URMILLA: One is enough for me, I could tell you. Is only a week since she born, but my hands full.

TALL BOY: They ain't full enough to stop you having a big birth night party tonight, though.

URMILLA: Is only a small thing to celebrate the baby, and the new job at the same time.

TALL BOY: That's all the talk now, working for the Yanks. I myself might have to make some changes...

[*A* WOMAN *enters the shop*...]

WOMAN: Reach half-pound of pig-tail for me, Tall Boy, I in a hurry...

TALL BOY: Don't be surprise if you see me tonight, don't mind I didn't get invite.

URMILLA: I don't even know myself who and who coming. Tiger like he going wild with the compensation money...

Later that night at TIGER'*s hut. The party is in full swing. A drunken hubbub of eating and drinking.* BOYSIE, TIGER *and* SOOKDEO *are talking*...

TIGER: How much compensation you get, Boysie?

BOYSIE: Enough to out off from Trinidad when the war over!

SOOKDEO: You best hads buy a taxi and keep your tail in Trinidad. A man don't know when he well-off.

BOYSIE: Like you, eh?

SOOKDEO: All I saying is the Americans and them would build their road and go. And after that we left on we own again.

BOYSIE: Don't include me in that 'we'!

TIGER: I agree with you, boy.

BOYSIE: Only you gone and get married... and you have a child on top of that, which cripple your style. You get old before your time.

TIGER: Who say so?

BOYSIE: You and me could of gone off together... You don't want to go to New York? And London? I hear it have trains there that does run under the ground! And this thing they does call snow that does fall and cover everything white, white... When I went to school the teacher tell me that if I go there I dead, it so cold.

SOOKDEO: Don't listen to him, Tiger. A man got to make-do with what he got. You try to eat the whole world and you choke yourself.

TIGER: All the same, I don't like this Trinidad we living in.

RITA [*passing by, overhearing*]: Since that episode with the doctors and them, you been having funny ideas.

TIGER: It wasn't only that.

SOOKDEO: You can't see is men talking here? You does wear pants?

RITA [*wheeling on him*]: Just let me hand Tall Boy this roti, I coming for you... Now, you old drunkard, you bring a present for the baby?

TIGER: Leave him alone, Rita. Is I who ask him to come.

SOOKDEO: Give she a chance. Let me hear what she got to say.

RITA: Tall Boy dismiss what Tiger owe him in the shop, Boysie bring a rattle, Deen give two fowl free for the party, and me and Joe give them money to buy a pram when time come to push the baby out... What you bring, eh?

SOOKDEO [*resorting to his learning*]: I was courteously asked to... attend this function... by Mr. Tiger, who *instisted* that I come... irr... irregardless of present!

VILLAGER: Quiet everybody! I like to hear this big talk! Listen to Sookdeo!

RITA: Big talk don't put food in your belly! Big talk don't give you clothes to wear! That's what he foolin' up Tiger with... All them high-falutin' words, as if that would help dig garden... If he wasn't here tonight he drunk as a lord rolling in the canal by Jumbie Bridge...

SOOKDEO: Woman! Your abuse falls on deaf ears... I have been nettled by children... scorned by adults... and relegated to the limbo of forgotten things in general...

JOE: That sound great... What book it come from?

TIGER: It have other things besides digging garden, you know.

RITA [*sarcastic*]: Yes, like America and England! Like Boysie!

BOYSIE: Left me out of it. I not no shirt-tail man like Tiger!

RITA: No wait! Is you who start the contention. Sookdeo say he educating him, and you for your part fulling him up with talk about America and England...

TALL BOY [*in a loud voice*]: What about a drink for everybody and forget the whole damn thing? I thought we was celebrating

Urmilla and the baby.

URMILLA [*shyly*]: Is all right, Tall Boy...

JOE [*clearing his throat*]: No, is not all right. I sit down here on the ground listening to all this crap...

SOOKDEO [*still in vain*]: I do not imagine you mean my dissertation, Joe?

TIGER: Wait. Wait. Joe is the judge. That's the best way...

URMILLA: I better take the baby outside. So much noise...

TIGER: Left she right there in the corner! She got to get accustom.

URMILLA: Yes, Tiger.

TIGER: Joe?

JOE: Suppose now, we make a plan. Forget all we been talking about... Suppose we say with all that money you going to make off the Yanks, that you build a proper house, like mine.

BOYSIE: If he want to stay home and mind baby, all well and good. But it look as if Tiger of the same mind as me. What you think, Tall Boy?

TALL BOY: It have pros and cons to any decision he got to make.

RITA: Urmilla is the one to ask, she is the slave who got to cook and look after him and the baby... What you say, girl?

URMILLA [*timidly*]: He is the man, and whatever he decide.

RITA [*snorting*]: Bah!

TIGER [*ironic*]: You think I could get in a word?

RITA: What?

TIGER [*ironic*]: Well. I like how you-all planning my life for me! Saying I should do this, or don't do that, or must stay here, or go there. You-all forgetting that I is the main one concern! And what I say is this: when the time come, we will see what happen. Is no sense scheming and making plans these days when it have a war on! The whole set of we could dead if the Germans-them drop a bomb on Trinidad!

SOOKDEO: Joe have a good idea though.

JOE: You got to plan for the future come what may.

TALL BOY [*trying to divert what looks to him an aimless argument*]: I remember when I was a little boy like Tiger...

TIGER: Who you calling a little boy?

BOYSIE: Ask me that! He have a child, man!

SOOKDEO: You going for more rum, Tall Boy?

JOE: What I saying is this...

RITA [*above the argument*]: All right! You all going to wake up the baby. Is time for the party to over.

BOYSIE: But is who giving the party, you or Tiger?

URMILLA [*aside to* RITA]: Rita, you think I should take she over by you? Is time for a feed.

RITA: Wait little bit, I'll get rid of them… [*Loudly*] Go on, Tall Boy, and you, Boysie! Is time to leave. Sookdeo, go and look for a canal to sleep in…

TALL BOY: All right, all right, you don't have to push.

BOYSIE: Yes, come on, it must have somebody else in Barataria drinking rum tonight…

They depart laughing and singing drunkenly. URMILLA *starts washing up.* TIGER *is sitting by the back door. As he talks with* URMILLA *their voices are subdued in contrast to the party.* TIGER *feels insecure and* URMILLA *is glad to talk, but frightened of saying the wrong thing…*

TIGER: Urmilla?

URMILLA: Yes, Tiger?

TIGER: Leave that and come sit down a little.

URMILLA [*joining him, sitting down with a sigh*]: I so tired!

TIGER: Yes… was a good party… Baby sleeping?

URMILLA: Yes, she drop back off.

TIGER: You wash that white shirt for me?

URMILLA: Yes, it press out already.

TIGER: Good. I don't want to go to the Yanks in the morning looking dirty…

URMILLA [*pause*]: I was just thinking…

TIGER: What?

URMILLA: What Joe say… About building a house afterwards.

TIGER: Joe himself getting like Rita, pushing his nose in.

URMILLA: Yes Tiger…

TIGER: Not that it don't make sense, in a way… The thing is, I have to decide… Boysie might be doing the best thing, maybe it ain't have no prospects in this small island…

URMILLA: You mean go away?

TIGER: Yes.

URMILLA: But what going to happen to me and the baby?

TIGER: We only talking.

URMILLA: Oh... Suppose we save up money, we might be able to build that house for truth... When rain fall, the ground does be so damp in the hut! It bad for the baby.

TIGER: Yes I know. You don't have to tell me all them things... You remember when you did small in Chaguanas, in the canefields?

URMILLA: Yes...

TIGER: And we start to get big, and we see all the old people around, doing the same thing every day. Cutting cane, planting cane, smoking a pipe in the night and talking and dreaming... Yes, dreaming. But they never do anything to make them dreams come true? I remember my father how he uses to say he would start a taxi service. All the time he talking about it, until people tired hearing him and start to laugh and it come a big joke. Worse, he still working in the canefields.

URMILLA: It good to have dreams though. *I* have.

TIGER: You?

URMILLA: Yes.

TIGER: What dreams you have?

URMILLA: I dream how if we had money, I would dress up pretty in nice saris all the time, and wear shoes. Shoes what have high heels, like Rita own.

TIGER: You just like a woman.

URMILLA: And I dream how we would live in a real house what have chairs to sit down in, and a table. And you know what?

TIGER: What?

URMILLA: Rita was telling me about a kind of electric icebox what does make ice! And you could put food in it and it won't spoil! She say she going to keep behind Joe for one.

TIGER: Them is just material dreams, man. What you want for yourself?

URMILLA: How you mean?

TIGER: Well... like when you lay down in the night and can't sleep, and you start thinking about life, and things you would like to do, and things what you have done already... and you keep wondering if that was right or this was wrong... you know how I mean?

URMILLA: I does only try to be a good wife to you, Tiger... look after you and full your belly... take care of the baby. I don't think them funny thoughts.

TIGER: Well that's you, but it's not so simple for me. It complicated. That's why you see I learning education... so I could understand better.

URMILLA: Sookdeo could read and write and yet he's a old drunkard what everybody laugh at.

TIGER: He ain't foolish like people think, though. He have something inside him... a thing like that, you can't describe it. You either feel it or you don't. Is no use trying to explain.

URMILLA: What it like? It like something to eat? Or see?

TIGER: No.

URMILLA [*with a soft sigh*]: I wish you could of told me... so I could change too.

TIGER: I not no different.

URMILLA: Yes. Not only me say so, other people. Rita put it down to all this learning business; she say you cluttering up you brain with a lot of stupidness.

TIGER: I don't see that. The more a man know, the less stupid he should be... You know something, Urmilla?

URMILLA: What?

TIGER: I getting a man. Is nothing else but that... You watch a tomatoes growing... or take the pepper tree by the kitchen there.

URMILLA: The bird-pepper?

TIGER: Yes, you could see it from here... You remember when it did small?

URMILLA: Yes, and it *squibbly*, like it going to dead.

TIGER: And look at it now, how big it get, and bearing so much pepper. Ain't is the same pepper tree? Only thing is, you didn't watch it every day to see how it getting on. Rain fall, sun shine, all sorts of things happen... and you didn't see when I put manure on it?

URMILLA: You did?

TIGER: Yes, that's why it get so big, and bearing wild! ... I feel people like that... if you don't learn to think and reason you stay there all the time, day after day until you dead, like what would of happen to that pepper tree if I didn't put manure.

URMILLA: I don't know... sometimes I get frighten because I don't understand. Is not that I don't want to, but those sorts of things you talking about, I never hear before... I won't have time to wash clothes and look after the baby and sell milk if I study them things!

33

TIGER: Well, maybe in the end you turn out to be the smart one and I only wasting my time… [*He stifles a yawn.*] Better go to sleep now.

URMILLA: Yes… Tiger?

TIGER: What?

URMILLA: I glad we talk though. It good to talk like this sometimes… Even though I don't understand I will still listen to what you have to say…

TIGER [*getting up and stretching*]: Ahhh well… every manjack start hard labour tomorrow on the road… except Sookdeo… Wish was my garden that didn't have to go…

It is a few days later. The Americans have arrived and the labour of clearing the land for the highway is under way. There are noises of bulldozers and heavy machinery in motion. The whole atmosphere is one of noise and bustle. A gang is working at clearing some bushes. JOHN, a young seabee, hails LARRY, another American.

JOHN: Hey Larry! Over here a minute.

LARRY [*coming up*]: Jesus, it's swampy over there.

JOHN: That's what I wanted to talk about… Don't want the same trouble we had a mile back when the land sank.

LARRY: And the heat! [*Swabs sweat off his face*] We must be on the equator.

JOHN: Just about, I reckon… [*Offers a pack of cigarettes*] Smoke?

LARRY: Yeah… thanks, John.

JOHN: We got orders about that swampy patch.

LARRY: Such as?

JOHN: It's our baby, like the local labour we're looking after.

LARRY: Huh… boulders might fix the swamp.

JOHN: Let's get more than that… Get them to dump all the odd stuff there… level out with the tractors… then tons of boulders and then level again. That should do it.

LARRY: That should also set us back a day or two.

JOHN: You worried?

LARRY: I only work here.

JOHN: Me too. Give the boys some overtime… Put the Tiger on the job.

LARRY: Hell, you must of planned this… Here he comes, now!

TIGER [*from a little distance off*]: Mr. Larry, chief? You could excuse me?

34

LARRY: I still see bush, Tiger.

TIGER [*now with them*]: Two fellars didn't come to work today.

LARRY: So what? I asked you for wizards with the cutlass, and you picked them yourself.

TIGER: Is only six of us there now, you see, instead of eight.

LARRY: Well, you get back there now and tell them there's only going to be five, cause I got another job for you.

TIGER: Whatever you say, Mr. Larry, chief... What other job?

JOHN: You want promotion?

TIGER [*eagerly*]: Yes sir!

JOHN: Then just do as *Mr.* Larry says, huh?

TIGER: All right, sir... Come back right away?

LARRY: Yes... [TIGER *goes.*] ... He's all right. Keen as mustard.

JOHN [*chuckling*]: I gathered that... Did you see how he jumped at the word 'promotion'? He actually understood it.

LARRY: He's one of the literates... been after me to let him do the time-keeping.

Two days later. BOYSIE *and* TIGER *meet on the site.* BOYSIE *has been driving the lorries carrying boulders and wears an American-style lorry driver's cap.*

BOYSIE: You-all ain't had enough of these boulders? I tired going up to Laventille quarry.

TIGER: You want to drive bulldozer, eh?

BOYSIE [*excitedly*]: That's the thing, boy! If you did see yesterday, up the road... they knock down a whole tree with a dozer. It was a balata tree, too... you could imagine. The fellar just drive straight up and tackle it. I must drive one of them before this work finish... You seen Sookdeo?

TIGER: I ain't had a chance to leave this swamp here... What happen?

BOYSIE: Nothing... I only thought you seen him... How much did you get for your tomatoes?

TIGER: Only twelve cents a pound...

BOYSIE: Me too... and you know the price went right up after we lick down we gardens? Old Sookdeo must be laughing, because he still have a crop... How you like the cap?

TIGER: It sharp, boy! Where you get it? I seen fellars wearing one but I don't know where to get it.

BOYSIE: If you give me a dollar I get one for you. It have a Yankee in charge of the stores who letting them have them cheap... You look like an American when you wear one!

TIGER: It keep the sun off too. Get one for me...

At TALL BOY's *shop one morning. Business has been booming for him.* RITA *goes into the shop to find* TALL BOY *hammering away as he erects a partition...*

RITA: Aye, like you repairing the shop, Tall Boy?

TALL BOY [*hard at work*]: I just putting up a partition here.

RITA: What for, pray?

TALL BOY: The Yanks...

RITA: How you mean the Yanks? Explain yourself, man.

TALL BOY: Yesterday a blooming coolie get sick and vomit near one of the Seabees and he didn't like it... So now I putting up this *barrication*... The Yanks in this corner, and everybody else over there.

RITA: H'mmm... contention start!

TALL BOY: Girl, I know which side my bread butter, *oui*... They spend more money in one evening than all the villagers in a week...

Later, in the evening of that day, angry VILLAGERS *in* TALL BOY's *bar...*

TIGER: What slackness is this, Tall Boy?

TALL BOY: I know which side my bread butter...

TIGER: You even buy new tables and chairs!

BOYSIE: Yes... He never treat us like that. We got to stand up at the counter and drink.

TALL BOY: After one time is another... Them is my best customers... paying cash on the nail too.

TIGER: And you mean to say, if Boysie and me and Sookdeo want to go over there and sit down, we can't?

TALL BOY: If a Yank invite you over... [*Begins to plead*] You boys know how it is... It have officers does come for a drink too.

BOYSIE: It have such places in Port of Spain, but this is Barataria, man!

TIGER: What get in you so sudden, Tall Boy? You even have special glasses and jugs over there...

SOOKDEO: Is because they white... You-all don't understand? White

36

people different from we... You forget what happen when your wife was having a baby, Tiger?

TIGER: But a man is a man... They can't come in we village and tell we how to live! I mad to break down this stupid partition! [*There are cries of agreement.*]

TALL BOY: I get the police if you do that! Is my shop and I could do what I want!

AMERICAN [*from the other side*]: Hey Shorty! What about some service over here?

TALL BOY: Coming sir! [*He goes.*]

BOYSIE: I never see Tall Boy move so fast!

SOOKDEO: Look, we have we rum and we drinking. For my part I don't care if I sitting, standing or laying down...

TIGER [*thoughtfully*]: I suppose Tall Boy got a point... After all is the Yanks who giving we work...

BOYSIE [*angry*]: What happen to the two of you? You taking Tall Boy side?

TIGER: How you mean?

BOYSIE: Well we is the village, ain't we? Why he got to separate we from the Americans-them? They don't buy no goods. They only drop in for drinks.

SOOKDEO [*patiently*]: I tell you is because they white.

BOYSIE: Aye, aye, who you calling black man? I is a Indian, not no nigger.

TIGER: That's not the point, Boysie...

BOYSIE: What's the point then? Them better than we?

SOOKDEO: Them white.

TIGER: You see, Boysie, you not educated. Now, education would teach you that the white man live in a different world... He does things what we ain't accustom to...not so, Sookdeo?

SOOKDEO: You right, and at the same time, you wrong. Is a matter of principle...

BOYSIE: Call it what you like, I don't like it. And furthermore, if the two of you can't see my point, is because you always arsing around with words and books, what teach you different things than what actually happen.

TIGER: Well Sookdeo say in America it have a different place for the white man and the black man. Which part the white man go, the black man can't go... Same thing in England too!

37

BOYSIE: You lie! I had a friend who join the RAF and went there, and he write home to say how the English people like him. He even thinking of settling there after the war finish! In fact I change my mind, and going to England instead of America.

SOOKDEO: White man country all the same, I warning you. You go to America, you go to England, is all the same.

BOYSIE [*stoutly*]: We is British! It different over there. We helping them to kill the Germans... My friend say how he only going to fete... free meals, free drinks.

SOOKDEO: That's while he wearing the uniform. Afterwards... and I making a big thing of this, because I warning everybody... when the war done, and peace declare, they going to treat we like the slaves we originally was... leastways the Creole boys! We Indians was never slaves and never will be! This friend... he Creole or Indian?

BOYSIE: Creole.

SOOKDEO: Same thing I mean... They don't know over there that coolie and nigger come from the same country...

TIGER: We straying from the point... We concern with Barataria and the Yanks... and I say, we got a lot to learn from these white people who from a different country... I for one done learn white man would come to look after my wife when Trinidadians too busy!

BOYSIE: It look to me like you playing both-sides. Which is all very well and good provided you know how you stand.

TIGER: On top of that, we got to remember is them who giving we work now... I mean, to come back to the point, you can't blame Tall Boy?

BOYSIE: Who talking, you or rum?

TIGER: I only had a few...

BOYSIE: I notice you, you know, Tiger, you friendly with your neighbour Joe, who is Creole... You favour the white man since that doctor come when Urmilla was having the baby... and with the arrival of the Yanks on the scene, you gone mad... Boy, we is Indians together...

TIGER: What the hell difference it make if you is a Indian or a American or English or... or... what's the name of those people again, Sookdeo? Who live in that place next to Indian...

SOOKDEO: Indonesians.

BOYSIE: Yes… well ain't that the same thing I arguing? Why it got to have separation in the shop for the Americans?

TIGER: Ah! But you missing the point entirely!

BOYSIE [*disgustedly*]: You-all full of… just because you could read and write… My money just as good as them Yankees across there, and if Tall Boy don't treat me the same, to hell with him! I go to the shop on the main road for my rum.

TALL BOY [*coming from the other side*]: I could hear your voices over there… Tell me this. Any of you ever drink with a white man before?

BOYSIE: The Yanks is only birds of passage, and when they gone, is we who support you…

TIGER [*tired with the argument*]: Ah-h-h… forget the whole thing and have a drink.

BOYSIE [*sullenly*]: No…

TIGER [*trying to ease feelings*]: I could have one balancing a bottle on my head! You want to see?

BOYSIE: I don't want to see nothing… I going home.

TIGER: You was for the Yanks from the beginning! What change your mind?

BOYSIE [*moving off*]: With all them big words you learning, you still stupid. It have things books won't learn you, and you going to remain a little boy until you realise Barataria ain't the world… [*He goes.*]

TIGER: Ahhh, don't mind him, Sookdeo, have another drink…

Later, TIGER, *still bugged by* BOYSIE's *attitude, calls straight to* JOE's *house from the rumshop…* JOE *is not pleased to see him…*

JOE: You been home?

TIGER [*argumentative*]: No, but…

JOE: Urmilla know you here?

TIGER: To hell with she!

JOE: Look man, why you don't go and eat your dinner?… Come over afterwards if you want to talk.

TIGER [*in drunken insistence*]: But man Joe is what Boysie say, that I traitor-rising our position in this village!

JOE: After you have a meal you feel different…

TIGER: I don't want no blooming meal! I asking you a question man to man!

JOE [*exasperated*]: What?

TIGER [*juggling drunkenly with a direct question*]: I mean… people got to look after themselves? Not so? Tall Boy right, ain't he?

JOE: Exclude me from all this ta-la-la in the village. I work in the town, thank God.

TIGER: But just suppose you got to make a stand…

JOE [*animatedly*]: Man Tiger I ain't have nothing to do with you-all! If Tall Boy build a partition that's your business! The question of right and wrong don't arise as far as I concern.

TIGER [*sullen*]: You just like the rest of them! You frighten to say you like the Americans.

JOE: I ain't like them… but I ain't hate them… is just that they here in Trinidad, that's all… A man got to make do with what he got… [*In disdain*] Frighten! … Me?

TIGER: Yes you! You just want to stay the same way… you don't want to use different word… or show a different feeling! And I know why!

JOE [*drily*]: Why?

TIGER: Because all of you want things to stay the same way! You don't want no change in anything… you frighten that the way you living all this time change suddenly and you have to catch a different bus to go to town, or you find the shop close when it uses to be open, or you can't get a coolie man to brush your yard because he working on the American road!

JOE [*coolly*]: You finish?

TIGER: No! This big public road they building… gasolene stations going to open up, people going to start building houses, the government going to have to do something about the state of the roads, with mosquitoes breeding in the canals… all them things what mean progress you frighten of, eh?

JOE: Look, Rita waiting for me to have dinner…

TIGER [*sneeringly*]: Go, everybody run from argument…

JOE: It look like me you is the one who frighten…

TIGER: I say flat out that I for the Yanks! What they doing is for we good… that road going to be the best one Trinidad ever had, going all the way through St. Joseph, and Cunupia, and down to the South…

JOE [*trying to make peace before dismissing him*]: Well you build your road, eh Tiger? Just let me have my dinner…

TIGER [*cooling down slowly*]: I ain't want anybody to get the wrong idea, that's all... You know I writing a book, Joe?

JOE: So I hear Urmilla say...

TIGER: Is not a book in truth, just everything what happen to me since I married... and all this business with the Americans and them... You don't get that feeling sometimes, as if you want to say some things what you thinking about?

JOE [*hastily, anticipating a drawn-out talk*]: Tell me later, eh? Go and have your dinner... [*He leaves* TIGER.]

TIGER [*as* JOE *goes*]: I ain't finish... [*To himself now*] These blooming people... nobody want to know what happening... but I going to put everything down so they could see and think about it...

A few weeks later, on the site of the road. LARRY *and* JOHN *are about to do some surveying. Workmen, including* TIGER *are digging and clearing the land nearby...*

JOHN: Don't trust just anybody with that theodolite.

LARRY: Yeah... [*Shouts*] Hey, Tiger

TIGER [*approaching*]: Yes, Chief?

LARRY: You stay with the surveying party from now on... in charge of that theodolite.

TIGER: Theo... what, Chief?

LARRY: Hell!... Just carry it carefully.

TIGER: Yes, Chief... I just want a minute to get my breakfast from the workshed?

JOHN: Ain't you had it yet?

LARRY: He means lunch.

TIGER [*quickly*]: Yes, lunch... We call it breakfast...

LARRY [*to* JOHN]: You seen that thing like a pancake they eat?

JOHN: Yeah... But I don't trust those cook shops in town.

TIGER: Excuse me, Chief... you mean roti, a kind of Indian bread. My wife does cook better than them restaurants in town.

JOHN: That's what I'd like... to eat a real native meal, native fashion...

TIGER: I could fix that up, Chief, if you really serious.

LARRY: You could, huh?

TIGER [*slowly, choosing his words*]: My humble abode is not a massive structure, but you welcome to come and have a meal...

LARRY: That's mighty kind of you, Tiger... What'd you say, John? You could write home about this!

41

JOHN: Yeah, why not? Sounds great… We could give Tiger some money…

TIGER [*quickly*]: I don't want nothing, Chief… is a privilege and honour, if you don't mind eating with poor people…

Next morning, URMILLA *is anxiously calling to* RITA *over the back fence.*

URMILLA: Rita! You there?

RITA [*distantly*]: Coming… just a minute…

URMILLA: Girl, if you know how much thing I finish to do this morning already! I even went to San Juan and come back.

RITA: What you went there for, pray?

URMILLA: Tiger came home drunk last night, because he get promotion with the Americans-them.

RITA: Oh? And you start to spend money wild, eh?

URMILLA: No man… is some sort of surveying work now… going ahead of the work gangs, planning how the road must go. I don't know whether they giving him more money or not. But that ain't what bothering me!

RITA: What then?

URMILLA: He bringing home two Americans to eat this evening!

RITA: You don't say!

URMILLA: Is true! He say I have to cook like I never cook in my life before. Grind the massala myself. Get achar, get dhal and make dhal pourri. Make meetai. Fry channa. Buy two fowl. Buy a new wick for the lamp… Girl, my head hot. I been on the go since I get up.

RITA: Well I never! He give you money for all them things?

URMILLA: Money no object, he say… you know how he is these days. That's why I went to San Juan to buy a new sari. He say I must look good. And I mustn't stop barefooted. So I had was to buy a pair of new shoes. And a new dress for the baby…

RITA: Like he gone mad! He bringing white people to eat in that mud hut?

URMILLA: I don't know what to do… I ain't even have chair for them to sit down, or table to put food on…

RITA: This time he gone crazy in truth.

URMILLA: Girl Rita, like you really have to help me out…

RITA [*hesitant*]: Look… I didn't want to tell you, but Joe ain't too happy 'bout all this business… lending and borrowing… you know how he get on sometimes.

URMILLA: I hope we don't cause no trouble between the two of you...

RITA: Oh, for my part you ain't no bother... is just that big mouth of his. I never thought to hear him say that you-all is Indian and we is Creole...

URMILLA [*embarrassed*]: I would make do with what we have... is only Tiger... He must be want to impress the bosses that he work for.

RITA [*snorting*]: Impress them with what?

URMILLA: That's just it...

RITA [*as if grumbling to herself*]: I myself, I don't know what I saying, because in the end I going to help you... you know that.

URMILLA [*relieved*]: Just this last time, Rita. I ain't have nothing! Not even a ware plate! I want glass, cup, spoon, tablecloth...

RITA: Whoa! You don't want a lot, do you?

URMILLA: What you could spare...

RITA [*with a good-natured laugh*]: All right, all right... But let me see what you buy in San Juan! Go bring the new things and you could try them on in my bedroom...

In the bedroom, URMILLA *is trying on the things she bought.*

URMILLA: ...Things so expensive! Four-twenty for the shoes.

RITA: You putting them on wrong... that's for the left foot.

URMILLA [*laughing self-consciously*]: I never wear shoes before...

RITA: Let me see you... h'mmm... They go with the new sari... Stop fidgeting! Look at yourself in the mirror now.

URMILLA [*in front of the mirror, taking a deep breath*]: I don't recognise myself!

RITA: Try walk in the shoes a little... they tight?

URMILLA [*taking a few uncomfortable steps*]: They feel funny... I should of bought a pair of alpargatas instead.

RITA: High heels suit you, you know... but your face look so plain. We got to do something about that.

URMILLA: How you mean?

RITA [*opening a drawer on her dressing table*]: Just now... Here. Try on some lipstick.

URMILLA [*horrified*]: Lipstick!

RITA: Yes.

43

URMILLA: Girl, we Indians don't put on that kind of thing!... At least, not me!

RITA: Ain't you want to look good?

URMILLA [*tempted*]: Well... you think I should?

RITA: Let me show you... Stand still... now press your two lips together...

URMILLA: Like this?... Take care Tiger don't like it!

RITA: Ah, to hell with him for once, man... a bit more... there. Look at yourself.

URMILLA: It look so red!

RITA: You don't look so bad! You're a pretty girl if you look after yourself...

URMILLA [*thrilled, but thinking of* TIGER'*s reaction*]: What you think Tiger will say?

RITA: You still studying him? ... In for a shilling, in for a pound. Shift a little, let me open this drawer wider. [*She takes out all her make-up appliances and plonks them on the dressing table.*]

URMILLA [*alarmed*]: What you going to do now? What is all them things?

RITA: Eau-de-cologne... powder... rouge... hair lacquer... eye-brow pencil... and this file to file your nails... Let me see your hands... I thought so, we could put some cutex...

URMILLA: But Rita, you like a drug-store with all them things!

RITA: When I finish with you, even Tiger won't know you!

URMILLA [*still cautious*]: That's what I frighten of...

RITA: You just sit down there... What happen to your foot?

URMILLA: The new shoes pinching.

RITA: Keep them on, you got to get accustom. You don't want people to laugh and call you country-bookie?

URMILLA [*with a nervous laugh*]: No... What you going to do?

RITA: First I pluck your eyebrows... Keep still!

URMILLA: It hurting, man! And besides, these is the eyebrows I born with.

RITA: You have to move with the times, girl. In these modern days every woman wearing lipstick and rouge... Why you shouldn't? You fall off a tree?... You might even be able to catch a Yankee soldier when you finish doll-up! [*She chuckles at her joke.*]

URMILLA [*uneasily joining laughter*]: You forget we is Indians and have we own customs and thing...

Later that day after work, TIGER *and* LARRY *and* JOHN *are walking towards the hut and* JOE*'s and* RITA*'s house.*

JOHN [*sounding disappointed*]: Don't say it's that bungalow?

TIGER: No, is the hut next to it. [*Thoughtful*] Well don't think my hut is the real thing, you know Chief... What I mean is, I poor and I live in a hut, but that don't mean everybody in Trinidad is the same as we. As you could see right there my neighbour Joe got a good house with all sorts of am... amenities... I won't like you to get the wrong *expression*...

JOHN: Hey! That's an electric light, Tiger!

TIGER [*with surprise*]: It look so...

JOHN: I wanted a lamp, or candles... or whatever you use...

TIGER: Well that light ain't usual, I can tell you... [*But he starts to play the welcoming host*] Come on, come right in...

[*They enter the hut.* TIGER *is quite unprepared for the elaborate preparations* URMILLA *has made in her desire to please him. He gazes round dumbfounded at chairs and table, glasses and plates and cutlery... He is stunned and angry, knowing the* AMERICANS *wanted a different setting. They are too polite to show their disappointment...*]

LARRY: Swell place you got here, Tiger.

JOHN: Yeah... yeah! Shouldn't have gone to all this trouble...

TIGER [*as if to himself*]: What the hell... [*Then recovering*] Just sit down and make yourselves at home, Chief... I will get the wife... [*Loudly*] Urmilla!

URMILLA [*from the kitchen*]: I here in the back, Tiger.

TIGER [*moving to the kitchen, where* URMILLA *has her back to him, tending the pots*]: Urmilla...

URMILLA: I just hotting up things...

TIGER [*angrily*]: Who tell you to make all this preparation? All they want is real food... [*He stops abruptly as she turns and he sees her make-up. There is a pregnant pause.*] What you do to yourself, girl?

URMILLA [*hopefully*]: You like it?

TIGER [*savagely*]: You look like a blooming whore! You going to sport in Port of Spain for the Yanks?

URMILLA [*on the verge of tears*]: I thought...

TIGER: And them things you borrow from Rita! [*Controls his feelings*]

45

... Afterwards. Afterwards you and me will have a little talk together. Right now I have guests...

URMILLA [*desperate to please*]: Yes Tiger... You want me to get the drinks now? Ice? Soda? I have everything.

TIGER: I didn't bring them here for any show... They want to see how we live...

JOHN [*coming into the kitchen*]: Got anything to drink, Tiger?

TIGER [*with quick recovery*]: Sure chief... I just seeing about it now.

JOHN: That's your wife?

TIGER [*awkwardly*]: Yes... This is my boss. Say hello.

URMILLA [*shy and distraught*]: Hello...

JOHN: We're causing you a lot of trouble, Mrs. Tiger...

TIGER: No trouble at all, Chief... some drinks coming up right away... You just go and sit down.

JOHN: O.K. [*He goes back to the main room.*]

TIGER: I hope you chop up the ice, real fine... What rum you got?

URMILLA: The best Tall Boy had. Barbados, Orange Blossom...

TIGER [*fiercely, as he leaves to join the Americans*]: You should of got Trinidad rum! Come on bring the drinks through... [*They rejoin* LARRY *and* JOHN.]

LARRY: Ah. Rum.

TIGER: Go right ahead and help yourself, Chief... just let me know when you-all ready to eat...

LARRY: Where's the kid, Mrs. Tiger?

URMILLA [*replying to* TIGER]: I take she next door so she wouldn't be in the way...

TIGER: You shouldn't of... Anyway, never mind. Go in the kitchen and keep the food warm.

LARRY: After she has a drink with us... [*He is helping himself.*]

URMILLA: I don't...

TIGER [*speaking for* URMILLA]: My wife doesn't drink.

JOHN [*coaxing*]: Go on, have a coke?

URMILLA: Well...

TIGER: Your place is in the kitchen, woman.

URMILLA: Yes, Tiger... [*She flees.*]

LARRY [*conscious of the tension*]: Hope we didn't disturb your routine... This was a crazy idea, anyway.

TIGER: No Chief... I just want to see you all eat and drink as much as you want...

JOHN [*proffering bottle*]: How about you?

TIGER: Just pour a little, Chief...

> [*They drink and exchange chat for a while...*]

LARRY: I can't resist that smell anymore...

TIGER: Whenever you all ready...

JOHN: How is Urmilla fixed?

TIGER: Don't bother with she! She going to eat in the kitchen... [*He wants to display his authority over* URMILLA.] You ready to eat?

JOHN: It's your party, Tiger!

TIGER: Right!... [*Loudly*] Woman! Food!

LARRY [*pausing slightly as* URMILLA *appears with the dishes*]: Boy! That looks good... What is it?

URMILLA [*shy, frightened of* TIGER]: Is bigan, sir...

TIGER: She mean egg-plant, Chief... You know it?

LARRY: Not dressed up like that... And this?

URMILLA: That's bhagi...

TIGER [*roughly*]: Stop calling things by Indian names! How you expect Chief and Mr. John to understand? ... Go and bring the rest.

URMILLA: Yes, Tiger... [*She flees back to the kitchen.*]

TIGER: Make a start, Chief... Just take what you want.

JOHN: There's... ah... room for Urmilla here?

TIGER [*deliberately ignoring the suggestion*]: Try some of this...

LARRY: What's it?

TIGER: Green mango, grind up with pepper and salt... and this is tomatoes, roast and mash up with onions and pepper...

> [*They sit and eat.*]

Later, after LARRY *and* JOHN *have gone,* URMILLA *has to face* TIGER's *suppressed anger...*

URMILLA [*in a quavering voice*]: I thought you wanted to make impression, seeing as it was Americans...

TIGER [*in full feeling*]: You do everything contrary to what I expect! They wanted to eat same as we, with their hands, sitting on the ground.

URMILLA: I only thought...

TIGER: You better stop thinking! You ain't got the brains for that! And another thing... What you gone and done to your face?

47

URMILLA: Rita thought…

TIGER [*sneering, taking out his own sense of inadequacy on her*]: Who is Rita? Your mother? You getting too thick with them Creoles…

URMILLA: I wash it all off right away, Tiger…

TIGER: Yes… and see if you could wash off this at the same time… [*He slaps her.*]… and this… and this…

[*He strikes her two or three times and she falls, crying out in pain… Next door* RITA *hears the fight and calls out…*]

RITA [*from a distance*]: Urmilla? What happening over there?

TIGER: Aha! She still interfering? Let me give she a piece of my mind… [*He leaves* URMILLA *sobbing in pain and humiliation and goes to meet* RITA.]

RITA [*seeing him*]: Tiger?

TIGER: Is Tiger self!

RITA: What happen to Urmilla? Why she crying for so?

TIGER: That none of your business! From now on you leave she alone!

RITA: Look at my crosses! What wrong I do to you, you drunk?

TIGER: Furthermore, come take all your fancy plate and silver spoon! We don't want nothing from you, we could buy we own.

RITA [*warming up*]: You must be gone mad tonight! [*Calls out loud*] Joe! Come listen to this half-pint man here.

JOE [*joining* RITA]: What all the noise about?

TIGER: Joe, you best hads tell your wife stop interfering in my business, eh.

RITA [*to* JOE]: That's the gratitude we get… [*To* TIGER] Must be the coolie blood… it got to come out in the end.

TIGER: And don't call me no coolie, you blasted nigger!

JOE: Watch your mouth, Tiger! You drink too much!

TIGER: If I drunk is off my own rum!

JOE: All that sucking-up ain't going to get you promoted…

TIGER: I have ambition! I could read and write!

JOE: And now you want white people for company! Was you going to let them eat with they hand if we didn't lend you spoon and plate?

RITA: And put them to sit 'pon the floor?

TIGER [*sullen*]: Was my business… I ain't have no quarrel with you, Joe… Is that cantankerous, interfering woman you have for a wife... go and decorate-up Urmilla like some whore in Port of Spain...

RITA: Well!... That's the last time. Look, I make the sign of the cross and kiss it... [*Loud smack as she kisses her fingers*] From now on you paddle your own canoe, come thick or thin...

TIGER [*with heavy sarcasm*]: Praise the lord!

RITA: The trouble with you is you too big for your pants. *Monkey will smoke your pipe* for you soon...

JOE: All right, done with all this... Tiger, go and try and get some sleep.

TIGER: *You* think I too big for my pants?

JOE [*half-humorously*]: Is a tight fit...

RITA [*with loud ridiculing laughter*]: The joke is... the pants he wearing is yours, Joe!

TIGER: I don't want nothing from you! Look... you see this? [*Takes out notes from his pocket*] Yankee dollars...

RITA: Go and buy some clothes for your wife, you cheap coolie!

JOE: Finish with this argument... You can't see he drunk? Leave him and come inside.

TIGER: Who drunk? I could drink more than you, Joe!

JOE: Sure, sure... Come away Rita... [*He pulls* RITA *away with him as he leaves.*]

TIGER [*muttering to himself when they go*]: I go show them who is man! They just jealous, that's all... because I writing a book... When a man try to better himself is so his own friends turn on him... [*He goes into the hut.*]

It is a few days later, in TALL BOY's *shop.* TALL BOY *has just installed a jukebox and* SOOKDEO *is inspecting it suspiciously...*

TALL BOY: Don't touch, Sookdeo. You could look, but don't touch. Unless you putting money in. And it ain't have no Indian records.

SOOKDEO: H'mm... And which part the money go?

TALL BOY: Up there in that slot... yes, just there. But don't touch, man! Is a new jukebox! Left it for customers who have money.

SOOKDEO: I got a shilling. But I ain't wasting it on that contraption.

TALL BOY: Well just read the papers and leave it alone...

SOOKDEO [*reading the list of records in the jukebox*]: 'Paper Doll'... 'They're Either Too Young Or Too Old'... 'Lili Marlene'...

'When The Lights Go On Out Again'… What sort of thing is this?… If I put my shilling in that slot, it going to play music? And sing?

TALL BOY [*exasperated*]: Yes, like a gramophone… You never hear of gramophone?

SOOKDEO: You don't have to put no shilling to play a gramophone

TALL BOY: It not for you, Sookdeo. Is for the younger fellars who like a bit of jive… Just leave it, eh?

SOOKDEO: It could give news like radio?

TALL BOY: Oh lord!

SOOKDEO: You think I stupid? Suppose now, just suppose, that I put my shilling in there and start to play music, and other people come in the shop. They going and get my music free! You think I stupid?

TALL BOY: Read the papers, man! See what the *Guardian* have this morning… I hear the Government going to disband the Home Guard…

SOOKDEO [*intrigued with the jukebox*]: Suppose I put in my shilling but I don't like the music… I could get it back?

TALL BOY: I just remember I got a barrel of salt-beef to open in the back… [*He gladly leaves* SOOKDEO *with a last warning.*] Don't touch it, eh. Read the papers… [*He goes out.*]

SOOKDEO [*hovers around the juke-box, deciding whether to risk his shilling. He reads the song titles to himself…*]: 'Rum And Coca-Cola', h'mm… that sound local… I suppose is as good as any other for a start…

[*He puts in the coin and the jukebox starts to play. Whilst the record is playing,* TIGER *dashes into the shop, out of breath…*]

TIGER: Sookdeo!

SOOKDEO [*excitedly*]: Listen, Tiger! You put a shilling in, and bam! music! It really work!

TIGER [*panting*]: I… been… running… They going to demolish your garden. Come quick!

SOOKDEO [*as the record stops, staggered by the news*]: What you say?

TIGER: Your garden going! Two bulldozers moving up on it now to lay it flat!

SOOKDEO [*disbelieving*]: Not my garden! I was there early this morning… Nobody tell me anything.

TIGER: Man, this is war-operation! Come on, you could save the ochroes and tomato!

SOOKDEO: I didn't get no compensation...

TIGER [*desperately, pleading*]: Worry about that later, man! Right now them bulldozer must be rooting up everything...

SOOKDEO: Oh Gawd oh! They reach the mango tree yet?

TIGER: Come with me. We got to make haste.

[*They hurry off,* SOOKDEO *already beginning to collapse with the strain. He gasps and pants trying to keep up with* TIGER...]

SOOKDEO: Wait for me, Tiger... I not as young as you...

TIGER [*waiting for* SOOKDEO]: Run fast, man!

SOOKDEO: They ain't reach the mango tree?

TIGER: Not since I leave.

SOOKDEO: I got money... bury under that tree.

TIGER: Here, hold my hand let me help you... What money?

SOOKDEO: All... all! I was going and give you, Tiger, being as I ain't have no family left...

TIGER: Well you got to forget it if they reach. When them bulldozer root up things they go deep and far.

SOOKDEO: Forget it... You don't know what you saying... [*As* TIGER *turns to go*] ...Wait... wait a minute.

TIGER [*stopping again*]: Catch your breath quick, we can't stop long.

SOOKDEO [*breathing deeply, in a broken voice*]: Is not two-three dollars I have bury, you know. Is two-three hundred, Tiger!

TIGER [*impressed*]: So much?

SOOKDEO [*wildly*]: All my money! I was laughing at everybody behind they back while I had it, and now it going!

TIGER: Come on then... just up to the canal there and we could see...

[*They run,* TIGER *dragging* SOOKDEO *along until they reach the spot where they can see the road-works. There is the sound of bulldozers at work...*]

TIGER: Sookdeo... we too late.

SOOKDEO: They can't, Tiger, they can't... [TIGER *restrains him*] Let me go! I got nothing left if they take my land and money.

TIGER: The only thing is if you get a chance to examine the dirt in the trucks when they cleaning up...

SOOKDEO [*broken voiced*]: You stupid, Tiger! You help the Americans thief my money! And it was for you!

TIGER: The road got to build, we can't stop it…

SOOKDEO: I got nothing left, nothing… Only death in front of me now…

TIGER: Don't talk stupidness, man! Sun bright over your head and you talking 'bout death!

SOOKDEO: Sun too bright! That 'dozer coming to kill me, Tiger! I warning you! You better stop it! Get the money quick before them damn Americans-them thief it! Let me go!

TIGER [*as* SOOKDEO *breaks loose from his grip and runs in the direction of the bulldozer*]: Wait, Sookdeo, wait! It dangerous to go there now! Sookdeo! Sookdeo!

SOOKDEO [*in a frenzied voice above the din of the machines*]: Come on 'dozer! Come on, you damn American thief! Taking away a man land! Come on!

AMERICAN: Hey! Watch it! Keep out of the way!

[SOOKDEO *rushes off into the path of the bulldozer. There are shouts above the roar of the machine.* TIGER *watches aghast, too stunned to move.* SOOKDEO *cries out in agony and the noise of the bulldozer cuts suddenly. We hear voices speaking disembodiedly as his last thoughts flash through* SOOKDEO's *mind as he dies…* TIGER *is left standing in shock… Voices…*]

RITA: Listen to this old drunkard…

TALL BOY: You forget it have a war on, a war on…

TIGER: I respect you… I will call you mister because you is a man.

TALL BOY: Rum, Sookdeo! I get a fresh barrel! Push your head right down in it and drink. Drink as much as you want, let me see you finish the whole barrel…

TIGER: That highway going to run through estate property in Barataria… Tell me how to spell in-ad-de-quate…

RITA [*mocking tone*]: Drink quick before the Yankees come…

TIGER: I is the only man in this village who respect you…

CHILDREN: Sookdeo, Sookdeo… you want a kick there…

RITA: They find him in the canal near the Jumbie Bridge, drunk as usual…

BOYSIE: I going America! I not staying here to suffer in the sun like Tiger, and end up like Sookdeo…

TIGER: I writing a book, you know, but you got to help me... I got a great respect for age, and you know what's been happening... First thing to put down is Chapter One, not so?...

CHILDREN: Sookdeo, Sookdeo, your pants all tear...

[*The sound of the bulldozer rises again overwhelming the voices until it stops abruptly and silence is held for some moments...*]

A few weeks later. The Americans have moved on with the highway and Barataria is trying to resume its former way of life... URMILLA *comes out of her hut with milk for* RITA. *They have maintained their friendship...*

URMILLA [*calling*]: Rita! I putting the milk on the back step.

RITA [*coming*]: Thanks, Urmilla... How baby?

URMILLA: She keep me up a little last night... [*Hesitates*] Rita...

RITA: What?

URMILLA: I know you don't like to hear nothing 'bout Tiger, but I so worried these days... since Sookdeo dead he worse than ever...

RITA: Well, child, you know Mr. Tiger is a man for himself.

URMILLA: I wish he did stay with the Americans-them.

RITA: Oho? He left the work?

URMILLA: Well they move up so far now... They ask him to stay, you know, but when he hear the estate people was giving new gardens he say he might try and get a plot... He himself like he can't make up his mind... On top of that he hear Boysie going England soon...

RITA: That's the way it goes... The Yanks come and gone now, and everybody got to fend for themselves, and face up to the same problems... I wish you luck, girl.

URMILLA: Sometimes as if I feel he would talk to you and Joe, you know. Is just that he shame-face after the way he behave.

RITA: We ain't got nothing against him, but I ain't dogging back, he got to talk first... [*She breaks off as a vendor passes.*]

VENDOR: Fish! Cavalee and moonshine!...

RITA: Aye! How much you selling the fish?

VENDOR: Two shillings for the cavalee... thirty-six cents for the moonshine...

RITA: You must be mad... You think I married a Yankee? Come let me see what you got...

In TALL BOY's *shop. He is removing the wooden partition.* TIGER *is there reading the newspaper... Passing* CHILDREN *tease* TALL BOY *now that* SOOKDEO *isn't there...*

CHILDREN [*outside shop*]: Chinee Chinee never die, Flat nose and chinky eye!
TALL BOY [*dropping board and shouting*]: Your mother must have been the Chinee! [*The children scamper away laughing.*]... [*To* TIGER] Now Sookdeo dead they looking for somebody else.

[TIGER *merely rustles the newspaper and does not reply.*]

Well... [*Dropping the last plank in the corner*] that's that for the partition... I hope everybody satisfy now... [*Pause*] Stop reading the papers and come talk, man. You want a drink?
TIGER [*his voice is serious and moody*]: You know I stop.
TALL BOY: Well have a coke then... [*Opening bottle*]... Is time you stop this slackness, man.
TIGER: What slackness?
TALL BOY: Well you ain't had a drink since Sookdeo bury.
TIGER: Ain't I having the coke?
TALL BOY: That ain't a real drink... You know what I mean... the way you getting on, as if the world come to an end. Forget your worries, man... You getting a new garden, not so?
TIGER: Yes.
TALL BOY: Well, just carry on as if nothing happen. The Yanks gone, Sookdeo gone... so now all you have to do is build your house and grow your crops... [*Jokingly*] and have some more little Tigers...
TIGER: You think it easy as that, eh?
TALL BOY: Look at me, I revert back to normal. The only thing left is the jukebox...
TIGER: Every man different. Every man got to figure things out in his own way.
TALL BOY: You only making unnecessary complications... Ah! Look Boysie... like he ain't working today?
BOYSIE [*entering the shop*]: Aye Tiger! [*He is in a good mood.*] I going to town to see about passport and thing!
TIGER: So you definite about going?
BOYSIE: I got my passage money save up, and who know when the war going to done?... What you drinking?

54

TALL BOY: He still on cokes.

BOYSIE [*coaxing*]: Have a rum with me, man. I mightn't see you after today. I got a lot of things to attend to, and I want to spend some time with the family in San Fernando before I go.

TIGER: I'll have a cokes with you.

BOYSIE: Hell! What sort of a friend you call yourself? Have one for Sookdeo, then. He would of drink with me.

TIGER [*tempted*]: Well, that's different...

BOYSIE [*to* TALL BOY]: Bring a bottle quick before he change his mind... and them new glasses you have.

TIGER: I didn't say a bottle!

BOYSIE: Let we make a start, anyway...

[*About half an hour later. The three of them have almost finished the bottle and are very talkative...*]

TIGER: ...and they didn't only give me a plot for myself, they want me to be in charge of all the gardens...

TALL BOY: And you just sit down in the shop quiet with all that good news?

TIGER: I was going to tell you by and by.

TALL BOY: The rum loosen up your tongue, eh? You see, Boysie!

BOYSIE: Ah, Tiger all right, he not a bad sort... What about the book you writing?

TIGER: That coming on too. I have Sookdeo in it, you know.

TALL BOY: What about me?

TIGER: You too... and Boysie.

BOYSIE: The thing is, what you goin' to do with it? All that crapaud-foot writing in them exercise books... For what? You can't eat it, and it ain't going to give you no bricks for your house?

TALL BOY [*facetious*]: It makes me sell a lot of pitch-oil for the lamp, though!

TIGER: You fellars don't understand... A man ain't only got to think of material things...

BOYSIE: Listen to him, Tall Boy! Ain't I say he would come just like Sookdeo?

TIGER: Left the old man to sleep peaceful... If you talking about me, Tiger, is a different story altogether.

BOYSIE [*derisively*]: You get stick with a pattern, boy, and your goose cook unless you leave Trinidad.

TIGER: Tall Boy, bring a fresh bottle, let me try and learn Boysie some sense before he go England and make everybody there think we foolish...

TALL BOY [*laughing*]: Who talking, you or Mr. Rum?

TIGER: Don't mind him, Boysie... What time you got to go to town?

BOYSIE: Well... if you getting another bottle...

TIGER: Good... now. You feel I stupid to stay in Trinidad, don't you?

BOYSIE: You stupid because you can't make no decision, that's all.

TIGER: I decide, let me tell you... *A*, I going to make back friends with Joe and Rita because I was wrong... Wait! Let me finish... I doing that because I realise a man ain't a man unless he could come out *frankoment* and admit when he make a mistake...

[TALL BOY *brings a fresh bottle.*]

Here... Fire one...

[*They refill their glasses.*]

BOYSIE: What again?

TIGER: *B*, I starting to build a good house to live in. With this job the estate people give me to look after the gardens, I going to make enough money.

TALL BOY: To pay the shop bills I hope.

TIGER: Don't make joke, I serious... *C*, which is the most important thing... I done with all this 'What happening, boy' and 'Fire one, boy' and 'How the garden going'...

BOYSIE: How you mean?

TIGER: That's the hardest thing to explain... but it look to me as if we always saying the same thing, over and over, day after day. I mean, like a man going round and round in a circle, round and round all the time... Even if we can't leave Barataria, at least let we talk about something different!

BOYSIE: Talk for yourself! I going England!

TIGER: Well that's it, you can't see? I would go too, but not now. It got a lot for me to learn, even right here. And when I good and ready, when I feel I could show myself a man to anybody, then I would think of whether I should leave Trinidad or not... Tall Boy, have a drink.

BOYSIE: A fellar like you who so studious shouldn't remain in this village here behind God back... Like it starting to drizzle, I better get to town quick...

TIGER: Never mind the rain... is only a passing cloud... like the Yanks.

TALL BOY: Hear you... that jukebox ain't no passing cloud, it there to stay for my customers.

BOYSIE [*looking at it*]: Yes, let we have a tune...

TIGER: We don't want no music, man, we talking...

BOYSIE: *I* want... Change this two-shilling piece for me, Tall Boy.

TALL BOY [*making the change and putting the coins on the counter*]: I get some new records...

TIGER: That blooming jukebox is the next thing to go! Men wouldn't be able to discuss nothing in the shop.

BOYSIE [*poising coin over the slot*]: What tune you want to hear?

TIGER: Come and drink your rum and left it alone, man.

[*But* BOYSIE *drops the coin. The jukebox starts to play 'Rum and Coca-Cola'...*]

BOYSIE: Look how calypso coming popular all over the world, eh.

TIGER: You will miss it in your new country...

TALL BOY: That was the tune Sookdeo was playing that day... you remember, Tiger? ... You want some more ice?

TIGER: Yes, ship some more, we got almost a full bottle here...

BOYSIE: I best hads be going... Like if the rain coming down in truth...

TIGER: Never mind, man, it good for the plants... You must write me when you settle down in England and let me know how things is... Maybe when the war finish I might make a trip...

[*The sounds of 'Rum and Coca-Cola' rise to blot out their talk...*]

THE END

TURN AGAIN TIGER

Characters

TIGER: Though married now for a year or so, Tiger is still a very young man, trying to find his way between the peasant traditions of his father and the wider world his reading tells him about.

URMILLA: Tiger's young wife. Her life in Barataria (See 'Highway in the Sun') has encouraged her to begin to stand up to Tiger and assert her own point of view.

BABOLAL: Tiger's father, still deeply attached to his Indian traditions and wanting respect from his son. He is still steeped in traditions of respect for the whiteman.

OTTO: The Chinese shopkeeper in Five Rivers, on the look out for a wife when the play begins.

BERTA: The young woman who is brought by Soylo to be Otto's wife.

SINGH: A canecutter in the village; Berta's lover.

SOYLO: An old Indian provisions grower and frequenter of Otto's bar, whom Tiger befriends.

MR. ROBINSON: The white expatriate manager of the sugar estate.

DOREEN ROBINSON: His bored and idle wife, who takes a perverse delight in tormenting Tiger.

VILLAGERS

SYRIAN PEDLAR

TIGER, *his wife*, URMILLA, *their baby and his father*, BABOLAL, *are on the way to Five Rivers in a donkey-cart.*

TIGER: Like this Five Rivers place really behind God back. We left the main road about a hour ago already. Is how far again we got to go?

BABOLAL: Not far Tiger. Just round that corner, by them mango trees, and we reach.

TIGER: Huh. You been saying that ever since we left Barataria... and this land in here don't look to me like it would grow cane... I mad to turn back. What you say, Urmilla?

URMILLA: What you think best, Tiger. But it too late to turn back now, you don't think?

BABOLAL: Wait till we reach Five Rivers and you will see for yourself. The cane plant already. All we have to do is keep it going till the crop.

TIGER: I only hope it ain't no hard work. Because I warn you already that I ain't here to do no manual labour. You bring me here in the bush to do the book-work, and that's all I intend to do.

URMILLA: Don't argue with your father about that again. You been over it over and over.

TIGER: This ain't no small thing. We left we own house and garden to come here to help him out because he can't read nor write... well not good, anyway. I just want to warn him for the last.

BABOLAL: You going to do the time-keeping, and any book-work that it have, that's all. But don't forget that I, Babolal, is the overseer.

TIGER [*scoffing*]: Must be overseer for them stupid people it must have in Five Rivers, but not for me. If it wasn't for my education, you never get the job.

URMILLA: You shouldn't talk to your father like that.

TIGER: Well, is true, ain't it?

URMILLA: I don't know how you could argue in this hot sun... phew! You want some lime punch? I make some before we left.

BABOLAL: Wait till we get by that corner. We go stop for a minute and you could see the village down in the valley from there...

[*They stop and get down from the cart for a drink and to look over the valley.*]

TIGER: Ah… that was good. What about the baby?

URMILLA: She sleeping, I don't want to wake she yet.

BABOLAL: Look down there… ain't it pretty? Watch them rivers going down from the hills.

TIGER: H'mm… what I watching is them couple-few carat huts. I could see only two house what have galvanise roof.

BABOLAL: One of them is the Chinaman shop. The other one is where we going and live… And watch over there, you see the cane.

TIGER: I got a feeling if I go down in that valley I wouldn't come out… Them hills might prevent my radio reception… You pack the radio good, Urmilla? I hope no valves aren't break or anything.

URMILLA: I pack everything good, don't fret you head.

TIGER: Come on then. We got to get settle in… and make the best of it for the few months we here.

[*They mount the cart again and set off.*]

The next scene is set in Five Rivers in the centre of the village. The LABOURERS *are waiting to meet them.*

BABOLAL: Aye, Singh. You got all the men here?

SINGH: Yes Babolal. We been waiting a long time, nobody ain't gone to the fields.

BABOLAL: Good. Now listen, everybody. These cane what planted in the valley is a special experimental cane…

TIGER [*interrupting*]: Don't use no heavy word what you can't lift up, and think I am any walking dictionary for you.

BABOLAL [*angry*]: Don't butt in when I talking to the men… What I mean is that this is a new kind of cane what the company trying out in Five Rivers, to see if it will grow.

SINGH: You mean like a new breed, like?

BABOLAL: Something like that. And we got to look after them good. That's why they giving the men in the village work, to make sure nothing happen. It have any of you who work in the canefield before…?

[*No one answers.*]

BABOLAL: …Huh! None of you! Well we can't treat this cane

ordinary. Anytime anybody see anything funny, they got to report to me right away.

SINGH: Like what so, Babolal?

BABOLAL: Anything, Singh. Tack-tack ants, blight, a tree stunt, or it ain't growing properly... anything at all. And especially watch out for froghopper. I go explain afterwards if nobody don't know what that is, but is a insect what is the worst enemy of cane. In fact, I will give a bonus to the first man who spot one.

SINGH: I think all of we understand. But you keep saying report to you. Ain't you going to be in the fields with us?

BABOLAL: Yes. I is the overseer, and I is responsible to the company people-them. And this is my son, Tiger. He going to take care of all the book-work... [*Proudly*] He could read and write.

MAN ONE: Oh! he got education!

MAN TWO: Mister Tiger, you will teach my child to read? We ain't got no teacher in Five Rivers. Tell him, Singh.

SINGH: That's a good idea. You could hold class when you ain't got nothing to do.

TIGER: I ain't come here to be no teacher, you know.

SINGH: You does drink?

TIGER: Try me and find out.

SINGH: Come, let we go fire a few by Otto shop.

TIGER: I will meet you there. I got to see about a few things.

BABOLAL: All right, men. I will see you later in the field.

[*The* VILLAGERS *disperse.*]

TIGER: Urmilla, you could go on now. I will go talk to Singh.

URMILLA: But Tiger, you ain't going to leave me to do all that unpacking?

TIGER: You could manage. But best take care of that radio. You go ahead with Babolal.

URMILLA: It too early to start drinking, man.

TIGER: I got to make friends, ain't I?

URMILLA: Well you better bring back some split peas and rice when you coming, if you want any lunch...

TIGER [*calling*]: Wait for me, Singh! I coming now...

[*They leave,* TIGER *in one direction,* URMILLA *and* BABOLAL *in the other.*]

Later, in the rumshop where TIGER *and* SINGH *are drinking…*

SINGH: …and boy, you like a one-eye man in a blind-eye country if you could read and write. This village like it lock away from the rest of Trinidad.

TIGER [*boasting*]: I ain't only have radio, you know… I got books. Plato and Shakespeare, and them fellars… you know?

SINGH: I don't know Shakespeare, but I meet Plato in Port of Spain one time… How come a brain like you end up in this village?

TIGER: That's a long story. I only here to help out my father. But though he ignorant, it ain't have nothing about cane he don't know.

SINGH: It have a fellow like that living up in the hills, Soylo. But like he hate cane and does only plant vegetables now. He got a garden.

TIGER: Eh-eh? I had a garden where I come from, in Barataria.

SINGH: You will meet Soylo one day. A old Indian scamp. He only come down from the hills when he have something to sell… What about another drink?

TIGER: A quick one, though.

SINGH [*calling*]: Otto! Otto! [*To* TIGER] That blasted Chinee must of gone back to sleep. He always sleeping. [*Shouting*] Otto! Wake up!

[OTTO *comes clip-clopping into the shop front wearing wooden-soled slippers.*]

OTTO: Don't make so much noise in my shop, Singh.

SINGH: Man Otto, why you don't stop smoking that opium? It got you sleeping all day… and now, with work in the village, you going to have a busy time.

OTTO: I ain't know why they don't plant that cane somewhere else.

SINGH: Bring a drink for me and my friend, Tiger, the overseer son, who could read and write.

OTTO: You-all finish off that bottle already? You worse than Soylo!

TIGER: Make haste, I want to go and see this house I going to live in. And you better get a pound of split peas and a pound of rice, while you on your feet…

Back in BABOLAL's *and* TIGER's *and* URMILLA's *house,* URMILLA *and* BABOLAL *are squaring up their possessions…*

BABOLAL [*grumbling*]: That boy getting too out-of-hand, you know. Just because he have book-learning he don't have to treat his own father like that. Is I who *make* him.

URMILLA: You know what he like. Just give him his own way and we would live happy.

BABOLAL: I going to have this room. The both of you could take the back one near the kitchen. Better for you to do the cooking. Let me help you shift the things.

URMILLA: Mind Tiger radio, eh.

[BABOLAL *goes out of the room and can be heard moving furniture around.* TIGER *comes back in...*]

TIGER: How you getting on? You got everything?

URMILLA: Yes... you bring the peas and rice?

TIGER: Yes, here. Babolal helping you?

URMILLA: He shifting the things to the back...

[*There is a thud as* BABOLAL *drops the radio...*]

TIGER: He trying to break down the house before we live in it?

BABOLAL [*coming back from the back room*]: That blooming radio so heavy.

TIGER [*alarmed*]: Is my radio you drop? Look at murder here today if anything happen to *my* radio...

[TIGER *goes out hurriedly and returns at once with the radio. He switches it on. There is some static and whistling. He picks up a station briefly with music, and relieved, switches it off.*]

TIGER: ...You lucky, you really lucky.

BABOLAL: It only had a little slip-down.

TIGER: You lucky, that's all I say... [*He looks around.*] This back room too small for me and Urmilla and the baby. You expect we to live in this cramp-up space? You better take it. I prefer the front one... It got a nice view from the window.

BABOLAL: You forget I is the overseer! I is the chief man in the village. I got to live the best.

TIGER: You *think* you is the chief man. Let me tell you, for your elucidation, that if it wasn't for me, you wouldn't be here. If I desert you, the entire estate will soon find out you are a fiasco. So you better make up your mind that Urmilla and me going to live in *this* room, and you relegate yourself to the limbo of the back room.

65

BABOLAL [*getting angrier*]: You being too rude to your elders. You not too old for me to teach you a lesson!

TIGER: You can't teach me nothing! You so stupid you don't even know how to control men. Listen to how you're going to give bonus to the first man who catch a froghopper. Next thing you know, one of them catch a froghopper from somewhere and put it in the cane to get the bonus.

BABOLAL [*enraged*]: You want to teach me my job too?

TIGER: Ah...h... Stop arguing and move the things.

BABOLAL: I going to move you! I will learn you to talk to your father like that.

[BABOLAL *squares up to* TIGER; TIGER *backs off.*]

TIGER: I don't want to hit you...

BABOLAL: Take that!... Don't run, stand up and fight like a man. Just let me get this belt off, I will beat you like a snake!

URMILLA [*frightened*]: Oh God, Tiger, you-all don't fight!

[BABOLAL *frees his belt and starts swinging it at* TIGER...]

TIGER: All I ask is that you don't hit me with the buckle of that belt... Ah!

[BABOLAL *strikes him with the buckle.* TIGER *is enraged and cuffs him down.* BABOLAL *falls heavily.*]

URMILLA: Oh God, Tiger, you kill him!

TIGER [*panting*]: I didn't want to hit him, you see for yourself. I keep backing off... He ain't dead... Help him get up.

URMILLA: You all right, Baboo, you all right?

TIGER: Lift him up, he only playing dead. I ain't hit him hard.

BABOLAL [*groaning*]: Leave me alone, girl. Is only slip I slip, else I would of beaten him like a snake.

TIGER [*calmer*]: I sorry, Baboo. I didn't mean to hit you, but that belt buckle leave a mark on me... Look.

BABOLAL [*getting up*]: I don't mind, that back room will do me well, Urmilla, when I sleeping and he come home drunk every night. Help me to move my things, Urmilla. Least you like a daughter to me. Just because he got education he think he is a man, but he got a lot to learn yet, I tell you girl...

A week later; it is payday and the cane LABOURERS *and their wives are congregated outside* TIGER's *house to collect their wages…*

MAN ONE: Aye boy! You have on new shoes! It squeaking!

MAN TWO: I got to dress well to get my pay from the white boss!

WOMAN ONE: What you going to buy from the Syrian man, girl?

WOMAN TWO: I hope he come and bring plenty nice things!

SINGH [*quietening them down*]: All right, you-all better form a line. Let the women and children stand behind.

MAN ONE: Where Tiger? He still inside, Singh?

SINGH: Yes. Sound like they having a argument…

> [*As they come out onto the verandah,* TIGER *and* BABOLAL *are quarrelling.*]

TIGER: …But you make me to understand that you was the boss! Who is this Mr. Robinson?

BABOLAL: That's the white man from the company. He living in a bungalow near to Paradise. You would of met him if you come to the fields to do some work instead of skulking about the village pretending that you teaching the children a-b-c.

TIGER: You never tell me any white man was here. You mean he is the one who really in charge, not you?

BABOLAL: He leave me in charge of all the field work.

TIGER: You get me to come here under false pretences. If I did know…

BABOLAL: Is this new kind of cane what they experimenting. They can't afford to take no chances.

TIGER [*sneering*]: And they can't afford to take any chances with the pay, eh? That's why he coming with the money?

BABOLAL: Man Tiger, stop arguing. He going to be here just now… Help me to put out the table and chair in the gallery… and bring the time-sheets.

TIGER: You better bring out a bottle of rum, too. Them white people does drink more than we.

BABOLAL [*nervous*]: You think we should?

TIGER: Well you got to entertain, ain't you? Show him you got manners.

BABOLAL: All right… but behave yourself, Tiger, don't let me down in front of the white people.

TIGER: Ah, you disgust me sometimes. I don't like this complex way you have. We not in the days of slavery, you know.

BABOLAL: Help me with the table...

[*They bring a table and chair out to the front of the verandah. There is a bit of slow hand-clapping and whistling from the* WORKERS *as they appear.*]

BABOLAL [*loud, addressing the crowd*]: Everything all right, Singh?

SINGH [*from the crowd*]: Yes, Babolal.

BABOLAL: Best hads line up the workers. Let me look myself... I hope you-all have on shoes... and listen, I want good behaviour when the money paying out. Don't start up no argument with Tiger in front of the supervisor, wait till afterwards. And no rushing and scrambling... Singh, you see that they keep in order...

[*There is a sound of horses approaching; at the sound, excitement mounts...*]

MAN ONE: The money coming, Babolal!

BABOLAL: Quick, Tiger, quick! Bring another chair! Like Mr. Robinson bringing he wife with him!

[TIGER *goes into the house to bring out another chair. As the* ROBINSONS *enter, dressed for riding,* MR. ROBINSON *carrying a money bag, there is an awed silence and the* VILLAGERS *assume postures of servility, murmuring respectful greetings.* BABOLAL *in particular is nervous and servile.* MR. ROBINSON *looks hot and irritated;* MRS. ROBINSON, *who is younger, looks indifferent and bored...*]

MAN ONE: Morning sir, morning madam...

[*The* ROBINSONS *ignore this greeting. They are concerned only to get out of the sun. They go up the wooden steps to the verandah.*]

BABOLAL: Morning-morning-morning, Sir, and madam...

ROBINSON [*plonking the money bag on the table*]: Ah, Babolal. My God, it's hot.

BABOLAL: Yes sir, very hot, Sir...

ROBINSON: This is my wife... I don't suppose you've got anything like ice round here?

BABOLAL: Ice... ice... I could send by the shop to find out, Sir, sometimes Otto get some from Paradise... I have a bottle of rum here... and glasses... Sit down, Sir, and madam... the time-keeper should be here, I just go get him... Oh... you here, Tiger! This is Mr. Robinson.

ROBINSON: Let's get on with it, Babolal.

BABOLAL: Right away, sir, I will dash by the shop and get some myself, and my son Tiger here...

TIGER: Stop saying so and go, man.

BABOLAL: Yes, yes...

[BABOLAL *runs off.* TIGER *turns to* DOREEN ROBINSON...]

TIGER: If the lady will just give me some room by the table...

ROBINSON: I told you you should have stayed, Doreen. You're only in the way.

DOREEN: And do what?

ROBINSON: You could have gone to the club in town.

DOREEN: I'm fed up with that crowd already.

ROBINSON [*brusquely*]: Well, please yourself. You'll only be bored by this.

DOREEN: At least it's something different, thank God. I think I'll enjoy it.

ROBINSON: All right, time-keeper... What's your name, Lion?

TIGER: No. Tiger.

DOREEN: 'Tiger!'

TIGER [*bravely*]: Anything wrong with it?

DOREEN [*exaggerating*]: Oh no, it's a lovely name... seems to suit you too. You must be the only tiger in Trinidad?

TIGER: Oh, we got a lot of animals in Trinidad. We got lappe, and manicou, and quenk... if you know what I mean.

ROBINSON [*sharply*]: Don't be rude, fellow.

TIGER: I ready to do my work, Mr. Robinson, if the lady will just give me some room by the table.

ROBINSON: There's no need for you to sit.

TIGER: I can't stand up and write in the pay-sheets. I got to tick off the names and make notes.

DOREEN: My! He hasn't only got a streak of insolence, he can write too! The first tiger I ever met who could do that.

ROBINSON: All right, Doreen, you've had your fun...

DOREEN: Don't talk that way to me in front of these people, Herbert!

69

ROBINSON [*weakly*]: Why don't you take a walk around the village, dear? Give me half an hour.

DOREEN: What's there to see in this forsaken valley?

ROBINSON: For heaven's sake! We're going to be here all morning!

DOREEN [*petulantly*]: Oh... all right... You won't forget about the gardener?

ROBINSON: I'll get Babolal to send someone.

DOREEN: This young man would do. Perhaps it's being idle makes him forget himself.

ROBINSON [*quickly*]: All right, all right.

DOREEN: You won't be long?

ROBINSON: I'll get on with it as soon as you leave...

[DOREEN *goes. There is the sound of her riding off on her horse.* ROBINSON *opens the money bag.*]

ROBINSON: All right, Tiger...

TIGER [*shouting*]: Rajnauth! Three dollars and ten cents...

[*In turn the men, women and children shuffle forward to be paid as* TIGER *calls out their names.* SINGH *comes forward as the last to be paid...*]

TIGER: Singh! Seven dollars and fifty-five cents! That's the last one, Mr. Robinson.

ROBINSON: Good... Here you are, Singh. [*He hands him the coins.*] Phew! Did you get the ice, Babolal?

BABOLAL: Right here, sir, waiting on you. I got a clean glass and a bottle of rum what ain't open yet.

ROBINSON: I'll just have water... [BABOLAL *pours it.*] Thank you.

SINGH [*aside to* TIGER]: Aye, Tiger?

TIGER: What Singh?

SINGH: Come aside a minute if you finish...

[*They withdraw out of earshot of* ROBINSON *and* BABOLAL...]

ROBINSON [*drinking water thirstily*]: Ah... now, Babolal.

BABOLAL: Yes sir, Mr. Robinson sir?

ROBINSON: Before I forget. Mrs. Robinson wants a man over at the house to clean up the yard and make a vegetable garden.

BABOLAL: Right away, sir. I'll send somebody.

ROBINSON: It doesn't matter for a day or two... You'd better send your son.

BABOLAL: Tiger, sir?

ROBINSON: Yes... and come with me now to the fields. I want to point out a few things to you. I'm not satisfied with the west section, you'll have to use more potash in the soil there.

[*They withdraw.* TIGER *and* SINGH *are talking a little way off...*]

SINGH: What you think of she?

TIGER: Who she?

SINGH: The white woman, man! She nice, eh?

TIGER [*airily*]: You mean Doreen?

SINGH: Aye! You know she name?

TIGER: Of course. Mr. Robinson introduce me.

SINGH: Doreen... Doreen...

TIGER [*sharpish*]: Don't call that name, before you get in trouble. Say 'Mrs. Robinson'.

SINGH [*amused*]: Like you jealous! I seen how you was watching she when they was here. Like a *real* tiger.

TIGER: You think I was frighten because they white? These people come from England and think the whole set of we ignorant and backward, but I not ignorant like the rest of you.

SINGH: Who you calling ignorant? If that's how you feel, I ain't going to tell you.

TIGER: Tell me what?

SINGH [*excited, lowering his voice*]: I seen she, Tiger, I seen Doreen!

TIGER: I tell you already, don't say 'Doreen'.

SINGH: Even if I say 'Mrs. Robinson' it won't make no difference to what I seen with my own two eyes.

TIGER: What?

SINGH: Boy, I even frighten to say it loud! Bend your head... [*He whispers something indistinctly to* TIGER.]

TIGER: What! You lie!

SINGH: If I lie, I die! It was one day down by the river... you know that pool it have on the short-cut to Paradise?

TIGER: By where all that bamboo is?

SINGH: There self! In fact I did gone to cut some bamboo to make a fencing. That's how I was there.

TIGER: And what happen?

SINGH: Well, lucky thing I didn't start cutting yet, else she might of heard me. I just get in the bamboo patch when I hear a splashing. And when I peep out, what you think I see but what I just tell you!

71

TIGER: Everything?

SINGH: You think I don't know a naked woman when I see one? You think they different because they white?

TIGER: Ah, you must of had a disillusion. You know how it is in the hot sun. She must of had on a white bathing suit, that's what.

SINGH: Man, I was near.

TIGER: How near?

SINGH: Almost as near as you and me now. You forget that bamboo grow right down by the edge of the river.

TIGER: And she didn't see you?

SINGH: In all that thick bamboo where I was hiding?

TIGER: So what you do?

SINGH: Do? What I could do?

TIGER: What *she* was doing then?

SINGH: What else you think but bathing in the river? And then, boy, *and then*, she climb up on a rock and lay down there in the sun. As naked as you born, Tiger. I seen everything.

TIGER: Every single thing?

SINGH: Every single thing! If you don't believe you could go one day when the sun hot in the afternoon and see for yourself... You want me and you to go after lunch?

TIGER: I ain't have time for that nonsense. I have my wife and child, you think I would look at another woman?

SINGH: You only saying that!

> [URMILLA *approaches them.*]

URMILLA: What you and Singh hush-hushing about in the yard, Tiger?

TIGER: Nothing.

URMILLA: You going to give me some money? The Syrian man selling some nice things by the shop. And Soylo come with some fresh vegetables.

TIGER: Come, let's go... You got to stand me a few drinks, Singh. I put in some overtime that you never did on the pay-sheet.

SINGH: Tiger, thanks, you're a real friend.

URMILLA: Drinks is all you study! It have plenty other things to buy... Is like market day come to Five Rivers...

Outside the shop, there is a noisy, laughing, haggling atmosphere as the villagers surround the SYRIAN PEDLAR *and* SOYLO *who is selling fresh ground provisions.*

72

WOMAN ONE: Look at this Syrian man today! He must be think Five Rivers is Port of Spain, charging a dollar for that hand mirror!

WOMAN TWO: He must be mad, we not rich people here.

SYRIAN [*shouting*]: Meester Soylo! Move your donkey. For why you take up my spot, eh?

SOYLO: *You* shift up with that bundle... [*Mocking*] Meester Syrian.

OTTO [*shouting from his shop*]: Aye Soylo! Best hads clear up that blooming mess that donkey make in front my shop...

TIGER [*as they join the shoppers*]: Here, Urmilla, buy what you want.

URMILLA: The Syrian have some nice silk. Get a piece?

TIGER: If you want. I feeling generous today... Get some vegetables from Soylo too. And tell him meet me and Singh in the shop for a drink...

Inside the rumshop; OTTO *as usual is lying down behind the counter...*

SINGH: Look at that lazy Chinee! He pull the canvas cot in the shop to lay down. Get up, Otto! You don't know today is payday?

OTTO: I just resting before the crowd come in...

TIGER: The usual, Otto, and plenty ice. I hear you got.

OTTO: One block, all the way from Paradise, Tiger. It got to last whole day... [*He puts the drinks on the counter.*] I got something to show you... Look, Tiger, see if the spelling correct. [OTTO *gives him a large piece of cardboard.*]

TIGER: You putting up a notice? What... [*Laughs*] Singh! Otto advertising for a wife!

SINGH [*laughing*]: In truth? What he have write down there?

TIGER [*reading*]: 'Woman wanted for wife and shop.'

OTTO: Please, Tiger? If it have a joke, tell me so I could laugh too. Is the spelling?

TIGER [*still in fits*]: Is just the idea of advertising for a wife what so funny, Otto.

OTTO: But why? I have plenty work to do now all the men in the village working in the cane, and a woman could help me out. That way I could attend to the customers better.

SINGH: Otto, if you get a woman to help you, you stick to that canvas cot like chewing gum stick to hot piece of iron, as the calypso say!

OTTO [*with a scowl*]: Give me back my piece of cardboard, Tiger. It not meant for men to see, anyway. Is for women.

SINGH: No, give me, Tiger! [*Singh snatches the cardboard and goes to the doorway and shouts…*] All-you women! Otto looking for a wife! Anybody interested?

[*There is a burst of scandalous laughter from the* WOMEN…]

WOMAN ONE: Who want to marry that sleepy Chinee!

WOMAN TWO: Otto don't know nothing about women, only opium!

WOMAN ONE: Don't push, Urmilla, is only for bachelor girls!

The next morning, in front of OTTO'*s shop.* SOYLO *dismounts from his donkey…*

SOYLO: Whoa, donkey, whoa… Why you so blasted stubborn? You hot foot for Paradise, eh, you have a jenny waiting there? [*He walks up the steps to the shop, walks across to the counter and pounds on it, shouting loudly.*] Otto!

OTTO [*clip-clopping hastily to the counter*]: Lord, Soylo, you frighten me… you mustn't shout so loud man.

SOYLO: That's the only way to wake you.

OTTO: So early in the morning? Cock hardly have time to crow!

SOYLO: You still looking for a wife?

OTTO: It look like I will have to get one from China. Everybody making joke of it in Five Rivers.

SOYLO: You don't want no stupid woman in Five Rivers, Otto. You want something better than that. It have some nice women in Paradise.

OTTO: I don't have time to look.

SOYLO: I could get one for you.

OTTO: In truth?

SOYLO: I going to Paradise right now… How much you pay?

OTTO: Pay? You want pay for that?

SOYLO: But look at my crosses! You know how much wife cost these days? Plenty plenty money. It have a shortage, you know, and prices gone up since the war.

OTTO: You know of somebody?

SOYLO: I might.

OTTO: I mean a good woman, a real hard-working woman who have brains and could run the shop. No old half-dead thing what you pick up by the wayside.

SOYLO: I could get a real nice one. She would give you plenty lil Chinee to run about the shop.

OTTO: Never mind the lil Chinee. The thing is, she would work hard?

SOYLO: The woman I got in mind is the hardest worker I ever know. She good-looking too. A creole, a born Trinidadian.

OTTO: I don't want no black woman.

SOYLO: You can't be choosy, Otto. The market hard for wives these days… but it don't look as if you interested? I want to get to Paradise, please God, before the sun hot.

OTTO: Wait. Which part she from?

SOYLO: She living there. I could bring she back this evening when I coming back. It would be a good match, Creole and Chinee, and soon you have little Ottos running about the shop.

OTTO: I don't know about that… but all right.

SOYLO: Good. Now to the business part…

OTTO: I give you a bottle of rum.

SOYLO: You ain't serious Otto, you ain't really serious?

OTTO: Two bottle.

SOYLO: Hear you! You think I wouldn't have any trouble? You think woman growing on tree in Paradise and I just have to go and pick one?

OTTO: Three bottle!

SOYLO: Three bottle?

OTTO: Yes, nothing more.

SOYLO: Even a case of rum won't be enough…

[TIGER *walks into the shop…*]

TIGER: I must be gone crazy, to hear talk of cases of rum? Men getting rich all of a sudden?

SOYLO: Ah, Tiger. You just in time to witness a negotiation between this Oriental and myself… you sort of get the idea?

TIGER [*catching on that* SOYLO *wants to baffle* OTTO]: I see what you mean… a negotiation, eh?

SOYLO: To wit, I do solemnly hereby declare, that for a certain percentage of cases of rum, I will negotiate for, procure and deliver to said Oriental one wife, irregardless of colour, creed and other incidentals hereintofor mentioned…

OTTO [*bewildered*]: What going on, Tiger?

SOYLO: And furthermore, by the terms of this transaction…

OTTO: What he saying, Tiger?

TIGER: You are suggesting, Soylo, that I become a party to the contract, by registering my presence at this auspicious hearing?

SOYLO: Exactly. And in furtherance, let me assure you that through the assistance of your connivance, by aiding and abetting, I do solemnly promise to compensate you to a certain percentage of said cases of rum… [*Talking naturally now*] if we could get them off this ignorant Chinee.

OTTO: Ignorant Chinee! I hear that! Tell me what he saying, Tiger?

TIGER [*laughing*]: You can't tie Otto up like that, man.

OTTO: Aha, he trying to tie me up, Tiger? He think I fall off a tree? The deal off. No more business. I don't want anymore wife.

SOYLO: We was just discussing the legal aspects, Otto! We got to have a contract, and Tiger here could witness. Bring some paper to write on.

OTTO: Paper! I not signing nothing. And I only giving you one case of rum, take it or leave it.

TIGER: Otto offering a gentleman's agreement, Soylo. You trust one another?

OTTO: You think I could trust this old scamp, Tiger?

TIGER: Well, payment to be made on delivery.

SOYLO: But you better deposit one bottle now, Otto. All over the world when men make bargains is the usual custom to put something down on account… not so, Tiger?

TIGER: Sometimes, yes… but you-all decide. I got to get to work. Otto, just reach a tin of condensed milk for me, and half-pound saltfish.

OTTO [*moving and getting things*]: A whole blooming case of rum for one woman… I mad to change my mind about the whole thing.

SOYLO: You see how stupid you is? She will have the shop looking new. So much business you won't be able to count the money… Come, Otto, is a long way to Paradise, give me a bottle to keep me company…

Later that night in OTTO's *shop. Outside, the sounds of hooting owls, buzzing mosquitoes, a barking dog in the distance, croaking frogs. Then there is a loud knocking at the door as* SOYLO *waits outside.*

OTTO [*muffled*]: Coming! Coming! [*He shuffles to the door and slides open the wooden bar and opens it.*] ... Who the hell is that at this hour of night?

SOYLO: Is me, Soylo. I bring back Berta for you.

OTTO [*sleepily*]: Go away, man. You wake me up from a dream.

SOYLO: I sorry, Otto, that it so late. But that show you the trouble I took. Berta young and nice.

OTTO [*grumbling*]: Come in... Let me light the lamp. [*He lights the lamp and peers at* BERTA *who is very young and attractive.* OTTO *is still in a half-doze and constantly yawning, not fully conscious of what is going on.*] ...This is the wife you bring?

SOYLO: Yes. Nice, eh? Worth about six cases of rum. A real bargain.

OTTO: It look like a little girl you pick up... [*Yawns*]

SOYLO: To tell you the truth, it was Berta mother I had in mind, but she gone and get married to another man. But Berta is real Chinese-creole. And she went to Government School.

OTTO [*yawning*]: I wish you did bring she in the day. You wake me up from sleep, man.

SOYLO: I want to sleep too... In the morning you will have a good look... [*To* BERTA] Talk to Otto, Berta, he is your husband now...

[BERTA *remains silent.*]

SOYLO: ...she a little shy, that's all... I will come back in the morning and finish off the business part of the deal... I will just push in the door for you as I going...

[SOYLO *goes out.* OTTO *yawns loudly. He can hardly keep his eyes open.*]

OTTO [*mumbling*]: It ain't have another bed, girl, you better sleep on the counter and tomorrow we go see what happening... Out the lamp when you ready, we can't waste pitch-oil...

[*He yawns and shuffles out.* BERTA *lies down on the counter and extinguishes the lamp.*]

Next morning in OTTO's *shop. A cock crows and the sound of carts rumbling to the fields can be heard. In contrast to last night he is very animated.* SOYLO *comes in.*

OTTO: Ah Soylo, I glad you come. If I tell you the dream I had last night, boy!

77

SOYLO [*chuckle*]: I didn't think you would of had time to dream!

OTTO: I dream you bring a girl from Paradise and left she here. Boy, it was so real, I never had a dream like that before.

SOYLO: It wasn't no dream… Where Berta? She cooking?

OTTO: What Berta?

SOYLO: The wife I bring for you last night! Stop making joke, Otto… [*Calls*] Berta! Berta!

OTTO: It ain't have no Berta here, as you could see. You must be trying to pull a fast one on me, Soy.

SOYLO [*alarmed*]: You can't remember? You can't remember how you open the door, and how we was talking, and when I left, Berta was standing just here… [*He walks to the spot.*] …Look.

OTTO: Well which part she is, then. You think I stupid?

SOYLO [*thoughtful*]: I wonder if she run away? She a little wild… She must of gone back to Paradise…

OTTO: This business with a wife is too much trouble, Soy. I think I send to China for one.

SOYLO: Wait, Otto, give it a try. I going and bring she back right now… What about another bottle on account?

OTTO: Not another drop till you bring she back. And don't come in the night-time, because I ain't opening the door for anybody.

Later that day. SOYLO *is returning with* BERTA. *He is having a word with her before they enter* OTTO'*s shop.*

SOYLO: …and remember, Berta, what your mother say. She say you have to stay with Otto and make a good wife. And you mustn't run away again, else she would send you away to live with your aunt in San Fernando, and I know you don't want to go there… Otto don't know anything about women, so you could get a lot of things out of him… Come in the shop now.

[*They enter the shop;* OTTO *is tidying up.*]

OTTO: I was just going to lock up, Soylo.

SOYLO: Look. Look for yourself and make sure you ain't dreaming. Talk to Otto, girl.

BERTA [*sullen*]: What you want me to tell him?

SOYLO: Tell him your name.

BERTA: I name Berta.

SOYLO: Say you won't run away again.

BERTA: I won't run away again.

SOYLO: Show him you could write... Give she a pencil and paper, Otto... Write your name... You see I wasn't fooling you? She could read too... Read what write on that package, Berta.

BERTA: 'One Minute Quaker Oats'.

SOYLO: You satisfy now, Otto?

OTTO [*a thoughtful pause*]: All right... I give it a chance and see how it work.

SOYLO: Good. Bring the case for me, let me load up the donkey.

OTTO: What case? You had a bottle already.

SOYLO: This Chinee man really mingy, yes. All right... bring the rest.

OTTO: I only giving you one bottle now, Soylo. And a bottle a day as long as she stay... until the case finish, that is.

SOYLO: We didn't arrange that! Tiger say payment on delivery, you forget?

OTTO: I don't care what Tiger say. You could take Berta back if you like.

SOYLO: Well... all right then. You got yourself a good deal.

OTTO [*plonking a bottle on the counter*]: Here. Now go and let me lock up the shop.

[SOYLO *goes out and* OTTO *locks up.* BERTA *is humming and examining the dresses and shoes in the shop. She intends to use her wits on* OTTO.]

OTTO: Now Berta...

BERTA: *Miss* Berta, if you please. We don't know one another yet.

OTTO: Oh...

BERTA: You got some nice dresses and shoes here.

OTTO: They come quite from Port of Spain... You want? Try on what you like... you is my wife now, you know.

BERTA: Not yet, not yet! Plenty of time to talk about husband and wife.

OTTO: How you mean?

BERTA: You got to prove you love me, Otto.

OTTO: Well, you could have a new dress and new shoes.

BERTA [*selecting a dress*]: I like this blue frock... Let me try it on.

[*She starts to change, la-laing a tune...* OTTO *gazes wide-eyed as he takes in her shapeliness.*]

79

OTTO: U'mm… ah…h!

BERTA: What you 'u-mming' for. You never seen a woman before?

OTTO: No… You have a nice body!

BERTA: You shouldn't be looking at me while I changing.

OTTO: But ain't you is my wife now?

BERTA: You don't know about these things, Otto. I will have to learn you. When people first get married, they have to wait a long time.

OTTO: But Berta…

BERTA: *Miss* Berta.

OTTO: All right, then, *Miss* Berta…

BERTA: Some women don't even talk or look at their husbands in the beginning, but I making it easy for you… Hold up one of those mirrors you have there and let me see how I look.

OTTO [*getting mirror*]: Yes Miss Berta.

BERTA: Hold it higher… That's better… it a little tight about the waist…

OTTO: Let me fix it for you…

BERTA: No no! You mustn't touch me at all; it would bring bad luck on the shop!

OTTO: Oh… It got a lot of things for me to learn?

BERTA: Plenty.

OTTO: Oh…You look pretty… but come, let we go to sleep now.

BERTA: The sleeping is another thing I will have to learn you. We can't sleep in the same bed.

OTTO: In truth?

BERTA: Oh, I sorry for you, Otto. I really sorry… I is the first woman you ever been alone with?

OTTO: Yes. I never done anything with anybody before. But I have a certain feeling…

BERTA: That is dangerous, you have to watch it and keep it under control.

OTTO: Well teach me quick quick what I must do and mustn't do.

BERTA: You must do all the work about the place. Get everything looking spic and span. Paint the shop. Get more goods to sell. And in the beginning you must let me do what I like, and treat me like a lady.

OTTO: I never thought it had all those complications.

BERTA: I will learn you quick. It look as if you got brains, Otto, and it won't take you long.

OTTO: All right. Tomorrow we will make a start on all that. But right now...

BERTA: The sooner you begin, the sooner you finish! You want to touch me don't you?

OTTO [*breathless*]: Yes! And...

BERTA: Well then... make a start from now to show me that you love me, and I will let you know as soon as it right and proper, when the time comes... You could cook Chinese food? It have a restaurant on the Main Road; I used to go there and eat...

The next day, fired by that certain feeling, OTTO *undertakes a series of activities... There is hammering, washing, sweeping, clanging... Outside the shop, customers, astonished by this activity, comment in loud gossipy tones...*

WOMAN ONE: Neighbour oh! What come over Otto, pray? He so busy working he hardly have time to tend the shop.

WOMAN TWO: Girl, you telling me! If I thought he would of change so much, I would of married him instead of Berta!

OLD WOMAN: Poor Otto! Somebody work obeah on him, or else is all that opium he smoking what turn him mad!

[*There is much laughter.*]

MAN ONE: Aye, Singh, you seen that little thing Otto get from Paradise? She got him moving like a bullet!

SINGH: And she not bad, she not bad at all. I done size she up already... She going to bring some life to the village... Ah, look Urmilla passing, I want to see she... [*He moves across to* URMILLA *who has just come from the shop.*] ...You been to the shop, Urmilla?

URMILLA: Yes, Singh. Berta is a nice girl, she and me will come good friends. And if you see how busy she got Otto!

SINGH: I want to see Tiger. He home, or he gone to the fields?

URMILLA [*sighing*]: I left him and Babolal quarrelling. That's all they do.

SINGH: What about?

URMILLA: Mr. Robinson want a man to clean up and work about the place, and Baboo ask Tiger to go. Well you should know what Tiger like now. He say he is a book-keeper, that he ain't going to do no labour work for no white people.

SINGH: Eh-eh! I would go if Babolal ask me.

URMILLA: It seem Mr. Robinson specially ask for Tiger. I only hope he don't go and cause any more trouble. Sometimes I does wonder what goes on in his mind, he like to argue so much…

TIGER *is on his way to the* ROBINSONS' *bungalow. He walks reluctantly, talking to himself.*

TIGER: …the only reason why I going is to show them… That Doreen must of ask for me to spite me for the way I talk on payday… She think I 'fraid? I going to assert myself, and talk to she man-to-man; I ain't going to behave like no blooming humble servant from the village… Lord, the sun hot!… but I don't think it far now… On the other hand, I could play humble and stupid and be laughing at she all the time…

A little later. TIGER *arrives at the* ROBINSONS' *bungalow and knocks at the front door.* DOREEN *opens it. She pretends not to recognise* TIGER *. She is intending to humiliate* TIGER *to cover up a physical attraction she feels…*

DOREEN [*coldly*]: What do you want here?

TIGER [*accentuating humility*]: I is the gardener from the village that the supervisor ask for…

DOREEN: Next time go to the back door. You ought to know better than to knock at the front. What's your name, boy?

TIGER: Tiger, madam, sahib.

DOREEN: Age?

TIGER: Twenty-two years old.

DOREEN: You don't look it… You know what you have to do?

TIGER: Tend to the garden, madam.

DOREEN: That is only one of the jobs I have for you. I want you to wash the car in the garage. Then there's the yard, all those twigs and dry leaves… sweep them up and burn the rubbish… there's the floor to be polished… Don't you wear shoes?

TIGER: Too poor to buy shoes, madam. I would be grateful if the boss have an old pair that he throwing away…

DOREEN: Well, you're to wash your feet before coming in.

TIGER: What else, madam?

DOREEN: The maid is in the kitchen, she will give you what you need. I don't want any gossiping with her, you understand?

TIGER: Yes... What do you want me to do first?

DOREEN: Start on the yard... [*The phone rings inside.*]... Just a minute... [*She goes inside to answer the phone, but her voice is loud and audible.*] ...Hello... Herbert? Yes, he's here... Don't worry, I'm going to enjoy seeing him sweat in the sun... Of course I'm bored, there's nothing to do here in the bush... Well, that's an idea... Yes, as soon as he's cleaned the car... I'll pick you up in Frederick Street... Bye... [*She returns to Tiger.*] ...Wash the car at once. You'll find some polish in the garage.

TIGER: Yes, madam.

DOREEN [*as he turns to go*]: By the way, aren't you the time-keeper for the estate?

TIGER: That's right.

DOREEN: It must be quite a let-down for you to be sweeping and cleaning! And you've lost your rude manners, I'm glad to see... Have you?

[TIGER *remains silent.*]

Answer me, boy!

TIGER [*unable to take more*]: You should know the difference between a man and a boy.

DOREEN: Ah! I thought there was some hidden insolence in your attitude. You object to my calling you 'boy'? Well, hurry up and clean the car, *boy*. Madam has to go out...

[*She turns and goes into the house, shutting the door on* TIGER *who is left fuming outside...*]

A few days later. BERTA *is calling on* URMILLA *at her house.*

BERTA [*calling*]: Urmilla, you home?

URMILLA [*from inside*]: Yes. That you, Berta? I coming out. I just finish feeding the baby... [URMILLA *joins* BERTA *outside on the verandah.*]

BERTA: She gone to sleep?

URMILLA: Yes... but don't talk too loud... Soon you going to have a little Otto to take care of, eh?

BERTA [*laughing*]: Girl, you don't know the joke! Up to now, I still have Otto begging and waiting.

URMILLA: Ah, you too full of mischief, Berta.

83

BERTA: Well is his own fault if he so stupid and he don't know nothing. I got him eating out of my hand.

URMILLA: You just wait until he find out!

BERTA: I even get him to hold a little fete for me tonight. Things so dead in Five Rivers.

URMILLA: What sort of fete?

BERTA: I invite everybody. I tell Otto that I accustom to a little fete now and then, and he want to please me so much that he agree. Singh going to bring his quatro, so we will have some music... You think Tiger would bring his radio, too? That's what I come to ask you.

URMILLA: That radio and them books he have like treasure to him, but I will ask... Should be all right.

BERTA: You must come. Tell Tiger.

URMILLA: *He* wouldn't miss all that drinking... The men in this village drink too much, if you ask me. You lucky Otto don't like to.

BERTA [*laughing*]: Is a good thing too, else he might get steam and have ideas!

URMILLA [*laughing too*]: As you say that, you give *me* one! I will try my best to get him drunk tonight, and then we will see him chasing you all over the shop...

[BERTA *goes, and* URMILLA *returns inside her house.*]

Later that night, outside OTTO's *shop, the fete is in full swing. There is much drinking and dancing to quatro music...*

MAN ONE: Aye Singh! Stop dancing so much with Berta and give Otto a chance.

WOMAN ONE: Give Otto another drink, Urmilla, let him warm up!

URMILLA: Like he had enough already; watch how he staggering. Go and help him, Tiger...

TIGER [*moving towards* OTTO]: Come, Otto, come over in the corner away from the dancers and rest a little.

OTTO: Ah, Tiger, I feeling dizzy in truth.

TIGER: Let's walk away a bit. Some fresh air will make you better... You only had one or two... Take some deep breaths, the night air will put you good in two-twos.

OTTO [*as they withdraw apart from the party*]: You right, Tiger. I feel better already... I not 'custom to drinking.

84

TIGER: Is a great party, though. We should have more.

OTTO: The radio you have, thanks for lending me… It expensive?

TIGER: You could afford one, only about twenty-five dollars.

OTTO: I don't want it for myself, I want it for Berta… [*He sighs heavily.*] Boy Tiger, if I did only know this wife business was going to cost me so much, and I won't get nothing out of it… Since Berta come, is only new dress and new shoes. She want to look the prettiest in the village, and only gallivanting about the place… [*Sighs again*] And the work, Tiger, the work! I thought she would of help me out, but in these days I working more than I ever work in my whole life… You had a lot to do when you first married Urmilla?

TIGER: Like what?

OTTO: I mean, she make you wait and wait and spend all your money and work till you dead before you could get anything?

TIGER: I don't rightly understand what you mean?

OTTO: Berta say I got to wait until the right time come, before we could do anything like true-true man and wife. I don't know about these things…

TIGER: You mean… [*He bursts out laughing.*] …You mean you ain't do anything with Berta yet?

OTTO: Don't laugh, Tiger. Is no joke… Everytime I ask she, she say not yet, not yet… How much longer I got to wait?

[*Tiger is still in splits.*]

Stop laughing, man.

TIGER [*gasping and half-laughing*]: But man Otto… Big man like you letting Berta wrap you round she little finger?

OTTO: She say it got rules and regulations… Look, Tiger, you mean I don't have to wait?

TIGER: What for? She only putting a set of foolishness in your head. She is your wife. She living with you.

OTTO [*dawn breaking on him*]: Oho-o-o. I had a kind of funny feeling that something was going on… I see, Tiger, I see. You're a real friend. I wouldn't have talked about it with anybody but you. Thanks, boy… I going back inside now.

TIGER: Wait for me, let me finish this cigarette.

OTTO [*decisive, with a note of finality*]: You might as well stay out here and enjoy the atmosphere, Tiger. *The fete finish!*

TIGER [*with a small laugh*]: Fete finish! Don't make rough joke, Otto.

OTTO: I say fete finish! You know how much that freeness cost me, inviting everybody in the village? All of them drink up my rum and enjoy themselves, and I only had a party because of that woman. I going to show she, right now, who is man!

TIGER: You wait a long time already, Otto, what difference tonight make? I ain't dance with Urmilla yet. Don't make trouble now. The fete going sweet.

OTTO: It going sweet for Berta and Singh, eh? You think I didn't notice how she been dancing with him all the time, and I been hearing things about the both of them, while she been putting me off. My blood hot tonight, Tiger, don' try to stop me...

TIGER: But listen to reason, man...

OTTO: Mister Singh bring quatro to make music, eh?

TIGER: What you going to do? Listen Otto listen...

[TIGER's *plea is cut short as* OTTO *strides into the shop. The quatro music stops on an abrupt note as he seizes the instrument. There are shouts of dismay... He smashes it on the counter, the strings making a discord. There is a sudden silence...*]

SINGH [*plaintively*]: Man Otto, why you do that? That quatro cost a lot of money. You got to get me a new one.

OTTO [*in a stentorian voice*]: Silence! Every body clear out the shop. *Fete finish!*

[*There are murmurs and cries of dissent.*]

MAN ONE: Finish?

MAN TWO: I told you-all Otto drunk.

OTTO: Order, order! Everybody go home and leave me here with my wife. Right now. Out of the shop, before I bring that chopper what I use for saltfish!

URMILLA [*in a low voice, awed*]: Lord, the drink gone to Otto head. We all best hads go...

[*The party-goers disperse, murmuring and shouting...*]

BERTA: But Otto! What nonsense this?

OTTO: You going find out *Miss* Berta. You keep your tail here.

BERTA: This going to set you back at least a week, you know. You let me down in front of all my friends.

86

OTTO: Shut the shop door... [*As she hesitates*] I say shut the door!

BERTA [*alarmed now*]: All right, don't shout... give me a chance...
[*She shuts the door, cutting off the noises from outside.*]

OTTO: Good. Now only you and me in the shop.

BERTA [*attempting calmness*]: I don't know what get in your head
tonight, Otto. You just had a few drinks and you start to get
ignorant in front of all the villagers... and I was just thinking of
letting you drop the 'Miss' from my name.

OTTO: I dropping the 'Miss' and I dropping you too... right on top
them flour bags!

BERTA [*as he advances on her*]: Now now, Otto! Remember all the
things I tell you...

OTTO: I find out you was pulling a fast one with all them nancy
stories, while you gallivanting in the canefields with Singh! But
Tiger open my eyes tonight.

BERTA [*surrendering*]: All right, just give me a chance to get change
and...

OTTO: *Now* for you! You keep me waiting too long!

BERTA [*excited half scream*]: Wait Otto! Not on top them sugar bags...
Otto... Ott-o-o-o-o...

A few weeks later. ROBINSON *is in the canefields with* BABOLAL *who is
some distance away.*

ROBINSON [*shouting*]: Babolal!

BABOLAL: Sir, Mr. Robinson... [*He comes bustling up.*] ...Yes, Sir?

ROBINSON: What's been going on here? Look at that ridge, it's all
crumbling away.

BABOLAL: Where Sir?

ROBINSON: Are you blind? And those plants look as if they've been
trampled upon.

BABOLAL: Ohh... yes Sir, I see now! I wasn't on this side of the fields
for a few days, being as we was doing some moulding on the
other side...

ROBINSON: You should be all over. That's your job.

BABOLAL: Is the men, Sir. They not experience growing cane, and
I have to stay with them all the time to make sure they do the
work properly...

ROBINSON: How did this damage happen?

BABOLAL [*angrily*]: It must be those stupid people from the village,

87

Sir. They bring their goat and cow to graze, and don't tie them good, and they break away and come in the canepiece.

ROBINSON: What have you done about it?

BABOLAL: I tried warning them.

ROBINSON [*taking a closer look*]: Look at this footprint here… What sort of animal made that eh?

BABOLAL [*as if to himself*]: Those worthless children!

ROBINSON: What children? You're not employing child-labour, are you?

BABOLAL: No Sir, Mr. Robinson. The canes getting ripe now, you see, and the boys come from the village to thief.

ROBINSON: You're very good at explanations and excuses, Babolal. When you came here the cane was already planted and half the work done for you. All you had to do was keep it going.

BABOLAL: I got a watchman, Sir! But the boys-them smart. When the watchman *that* side, they thief *this* side.

ROBINSON: Get two watchmen then. Or three or four, I don't care. And let them keep a day and night watch.

BABOLAL: Right away, Mr. Robinson-sir.

ROBINSON: Tell them if it happens again, they will be instantly dismissed, the lot of them. And let me warn you, Babolal, the cane has to be carefully watched at this stage. Thank goodness we haven't had any froghoppers. We've only got a 'few more weeks, and if anything goes wrong, I will hold you personally responsible. Not only that. I will see that you don't ever get employment on any sugar estate on the island. Understood?

BABOLAL: I will watchman myself, Sir. I will get some bad dogs for the watchmen, sir.

ROBINSON [*wiping face*]: Whew… it's hot… you think the rain will keep off?

BABOLAL: It look so, Sir… three-four weeks again, I think.

ROBINSON: That's all the time we need… Altogether I'm not entirely dissatisfied with the way you've carried on…

BABOLAL [*fawning, talking fast*]: Thank you, Mr. Robinson, Sir… is a lot of hard work, being as the men not used to working in the cane and I have to teach them everything, and I can't be all over at the same time, that's why these canes here damage, but I promise it won't happen again. I will get a shotgun and shoot down anybody I catch trespassing, man, woman or child….

Next morning in OTTO's *shop,* BERTA *is serving* URMILLA.

BERTA: …That's all you want, Urmilla?

URMILLA: Yes girl… oh, and a bottle of cooking oil… [*As* BERTA *gets it*] Otto still sleeping?

BERTA: What you think? If you smell the back room with the opium he does smoke!

URMILLA: Well, it better than the rum, I think. These men does drink so much.

BERTA: You should of heard Tiger and Soylo in the shop last night. So much noise they keep…

[SINGH *comes into the shop with a heavy package.*]

SINGH [*putting down the package on the counter*]: Phew it heavy! I meet a man from Paradise bringing it for Otto, so as I passing by the shop I bring it for him… He sleeping?

BERTA [*shouting*]: Otto! look a parcel for you.

OTTO [*from a distance, grumbling and swearing*]: I'm coming… [*Yawns*] What is it?

BERTA: Open it up and see…

OTTO: I didn't order anything. [*He removes the paper and packing.*]

SINGH: Radio, eh? You buying radio and up to now you ain't pay me for my quatro that you break up!

BERTA [*delighted*]: Is a big one, bigger than Tiger one!

SINGH: Go on, Berta, see if it could pick up some stations.

BERTA: It got so many knobs… I wonder which one?

URMILLA: Look, it have a little book there… Maybe it tell you?

BERTA: Let me see…

[*They are all waiting as she reads.*]

H'mm, I don't understand… better wait till Tiger come.

OTTO: Give me a chance. I will operate it… [*He clicks on all the knobs…*]

[*Suddenly Singh bursts out laughing.*]

Why you laugh, Singh? You see a joke?

SINGH: What I see is that's a sharp radio, but it can't work. It got to have electric current.

OTTO: I tell them to send everything. They must of sent the current too.

BERTA: It ain't have no current in Five Rivers, Otto!

OTTO [*searching box*]: I know, I know, you think I stupid? That's why I tell them to send it... but like those blasted vagabonds forget.

BERTA: No, Otto. You see this plug here? That's to put in a socket, like what give electric light.

URMILLA: Yes, you should of got one like Tiger what work off of batteries.

OTTO: Take it back, Singh.

SINGH: Me! I only do you a favour bringing it. The man must of gone back from the village by now.

BERTA: Don't send it back, Otto. It so new and shiny!

OTTO: You want to buy it, Singh?

SINGH: Yes, but not now. I will wait till the Government put current in Five Rivers!

OTTO [*grumbling*]: Put it up on that shelf, Berta... When Soylo going to Paradise I will get him to change it... [*As he is going out*] And don't wake me up for any more stupidness... Those blooming scamps, I would report them to the police...

SINGH: Berta, doo-doo, bring a drink for me.

URMILLA: I going, Berta. I want some vegetables from Soylo.

BERTA: All right, girl. I will pass by you later if I get a chance.

Later that evening in TIGER*'s and* URMILLA*'s cottage.* TIGER *has just returned.*

TIGER: Urmilla! What you got to eat? I hungry.

URMILLA: You not going to wait for Babolal?

TIGER: He ain't coming now, man. He frighten to leave the canepiece since Mr. Robinson take a turn on him.

URMILLA: I got chicken curry. And I get some nice egg-plants from Soylo... I got to hot up the food though, you don't mind?

TIGER: No. I got some work to do on the time-sheets.

URMILLA: Don't strain your eyes... You want me to bring you the big lamp from the kitchen?

TIGER: Is all right, I could manage with this one... I'll turn up the wick a little.

URMILLA: You seen Otto radio?

TIGER: Yes.

URMILLA [*pause*]: How long again we going to remain in Five Rivers, Tiger? Almost three months gone...

TIGER [*engrossed*]: U'mm… only a few weeks…

URMILLA [*pause*]: The cane already cut?

TIGER: Almost.

URMILLA: I need some bamboo bad to prop up those tomatoes I have growing in the back… You hearing me?

TIGER: Yes.

URMILLA: Ain't you does pass by the bamboo patch to get to Mr. Robinson house? You could cut some for me when you coming back tomorrow, please God… You hearing?

TIGER [*irritably*]: You think I deaf?

URMILLA: Well, you not answering!

TIGER: All right, all right… I will finish this work later. The food ready?

URMILLA: Yes… Just let me dish out some and put some aside for Babolal…

Next morning, TIGER *is working in the* ROBINSONS' *yard. The* ROBINSONS *are having a last cup of coffee after breakfast.*

DOREEN: Do you have to go out again this morning, Herbert?

ROBINSON: I told you dear. They're testing the cane juice at the lab. If the sucrose content is high enough, we may be able to get out of here quicker than we thought.

DOREEN: How long is that?

ROBINSON: Say, three weeks.

DOREEN [*pleased*]: As soon as that?

ROBINSON: A lot depends on the weather, though. They can't harvest the crop if it rains. But the dry season is still on… You going to town?

DOREEN: I can't very well if you're using the car… I suppose I'll have to potter about the place with that insolent boy.

ROBINSON: You asked for him, didn't you?

DOREEN: I know I did… I'm just being idle, really, trying to put him in his place. Maybe I'm being cruel.

ROBINSON: There's no earthly reason why you can't have somebody else.

DOREEN: I rather enjoy his company, in a perverse sort of way… Do you know, he had the cheek yesterday to move the drawing-room chairs around while he was polishing the floor?

ROBINSON: Probably forgot to put them back.

DOREEN: Oh no, it was deliberate. And that's only one thing...

ROBINSON [*interrupting*]: Yes... Well, I'd better be going.

DOREEN: Don't forget we're having Janet and Bob for bridge this evening.

ROBINSON: I'll be back in time for that... 'Bye dear.

[*He goes out. A car door opens and slams shut and the car drives off on the gravelled road...*]

Later in the morning, DOREEN *has the radio on with local music. She is bored, with nothing to do, and is drinking. She fills another glass and switches the radio off.*

DOREEN [*to herself*]: My God, it's hot in here... [*She moves to open a window, but it is stuck. She taps the glass to draw* TIGER's *attention.*] ...Damn! This window is always jammed... [*Loudly*] Boy! This window's stuck again. Try to open it from the outside...

[*Tiger opens the window.*]

That's better... ah, a breeze!

TIGER: I got to get some manure for these roses, madam.

DOREEN [*taking a swig from her glass; she is a little drunk*]: Damn the roses. I shan't be here to see them bloom.

TIGER: Whatever you like, madam.

DOREEN [*annoyed*]: You don't have to reply to everything I say, boy. Learn to hold your tongue.

TIGER [*ready for a showdown after weeks of taunting*]: I think you and me better have an understanding, Mrs. Robinson. In the first place, I got a name, and it ain't 'boy'.

DOREEN: How dare you talk to me that way?

TIGER: In the second place, we not in the old colonial days no more, when the white man crack a whip and the native jump to do his bidding... them days finish forever.

DOREEN: Do you realise I could have you flogged for this insolence?

TIGER: That's where you wrong, Mrs. Robinson. You could get me fired from the job, that's all. And it don't make no difference to me one way or the other. I already decide to quit, but I been waiting to tell you this.

DOREEN: You can leave this very minute!

TIGER: I might as well finish off the halfday, to even up the pay-sheets, I don't want to cheat the Company.

DOREEN: Well! You haven't heard the last of it, *boy*. I'll make you pay for your insubordination if it's the last thing I do. [*She slams the window shut, and then laughs softly to herself...*] ...Oh, he's priceless! I can't wait to tell Janet... [*She moves to the phone and dials...*] Hello? Janet?... Yes... fine, thank you... My dear, you remember our yard-boy... yes, full of spirit this morning... [*Imitates* TIGER] 'We not in the old colonial days no more...' [*Laughs*] What? Yes, I really must, I've been so beastly, but it helped to relieve the tedium... oh, I don't know. It's so hot. I'll probably go for a swim after lunch... Yes... Don't be late this evening...

Later, down by the river, TIGER *enters the bamboo patch to cut some canes for* URMILLA.

TIGER [*muttering to himself*]: I can't remember what bamboo Urmilla say she want, if is a branch or a long piece... Better cut down this tall one... [*He is about to start cutting when he hears a woman's voice humming distantly.*] I wonder who... Lord! It must be Doreen! But it don't have to be she? It could be somebody else... I'll just take a look and see, just to make sure... Lord is sheself! Singh was right... She sunbathing there on that rock... She got her eyes closed and... What is that thing? Crawling there on the rock... Oh God! [*Shouting out in alarm*] Don't move! Whatever you do don't move! At all at all! A poison coral snake near to you...

[TIGER *splashes into the river and dashes to the rock. There is a smashing sound as he kills the snake with the flat of his cutlass blade... He pants from the exertion.* DOREEN *sits up in a panic.*]

DOREEN: Oh... How horrible!
TIGER: Is all right. It dead now.
DOREEN: Oh... I... Tiger... My clothes!... Tiger...

[*The sound of the river magnifies into a roar...*]

Two weeks later, the WORKERS *are firing the fields in preparation for the harvest. There are shouts and warnings...*

MAN ONE: Watch it that side!
MAN TWO: Mind you burn yourself so near, man!
BABOLAL: Get round to the west field, Singh! You and Rajnauth!

...Watch for the wind! Keep an eye on that corner over there! Tiger! Things all right over by you?

TIGER [*distantly*]: Yes. But you better send a man to relieve me. I been here six hours. I want a break.

BABOLAL: Stop Singh as he passing then! And when you had a rest, check how they controlling the west side for me...

Back in the village, URMILLA *and* BERTA *are out in the road watching the sky.*

URMILLA: This is the first time you seeing them burn cane, Berta?

BERTA: I never been in a village so near before! We could hear the fire from here in the road... and watch how red the sky is!

URMILLA: That's the only time Tiger like... when they burning the cane... that's why he's gone to help Babolal.

BERTA: If you ask me, every man in the village gone to help... and you could imagine the ruction in the shop tonight when they come to drink!

URMILLA [*struck by an idea*]: Listen! As you say that, now is the best time to do it. Let we get all the women together, and see if they agree to this idea...

Later, a gathering of all the WOMEN *in Five Rivers...*

BERTA [*loudly*]: All right! Urmilla have to be spokesman, because it don't look good for me, being Otto's wife, to be the leader. Now is a good time to go and see him, as all the men in the fields burning the cane. Otto sitting in the gallery.

WOMAN ONE: I don't know if we husbands going to like what we doing, eh Urmilla?

URMILLA: Is for their own sakes. They will all become drunkards if we don't do something. Come on, everybody...

[*The* WOMEN *set off together for the rum shop.* OTTO *sees them approaching...*]

OTTO [*musing to himself*]: Look at all them women coming down the road, I wonder which part they going? Must be to wash clothes in the river... [*Alert voice now*] A-ah! Like they coming here!

[*The group stops in front of the rum shop.*]

URMILLA: Otto!

OTTO [*chuckling*]: You see how you women is? The first chance all the men gone to work in the cane, and you-all come to Otto! But I can't take on the whole set at one time!

URMILLA: Keep quiet and listen, Otto. We tired of the men getting drunk every night. And as you see, all the women here, and we say that you got to stop giving them rum on credit. Right girls?

[*There are shouts of agreement and cheers.*]

OTTO: Who put you up to this nonsense, Urmilla? Couldn't be Tiger! I bet you is Berta... I could see she head in the crowd!

URMILLA: We women make up our own minds; it didn't have nothing to do with Berta.

OTTO: To tell you the truth, I don't mind, Urmilla. Is only the rum they drinking what making me keep the shop open late at night, when I could be with my darling Berta...

[*There is tittering from the women...*]

BERTA: Don't get fresh with me in front of the women, Otto! I could still put you back on probation!

[*There is loud laughter...*]

URMILLA: Let we get serious. I want Otto to agree.

OTTO: Well, if they ask me anything, I will say that you-all threaten to beat me up and stop buying from the shop.

URMILLA: At least it would show them that we have feelings too.

WOMAN ONE: Yes, girl Urmilla, and give we some time with the children instead of sapping their heads with soda-water and running to hot up the food at all hours of the night...

Later that evening, TIGER *and* SINGH *are walking to the shop after a hard evening burning the canes...*

SINGH [*catching up with* TIGER]: Wait for me Tiger! You walking so fast.

TIGER: Come on then. After all that work I feel like a bottle.

SINGH: Well is only a few more yards to the shop...

[*As they arrive there they find a crowd of men milling around outside talking angrily.*]

MAN ONE: Tiger! See if you could talk sense to this crazy Chinee. He say no more rum on credit!

MAN TWO: Ah yes, look Tiger come, Otto! Let we see if you will treat him the same way.

OTTO: He is the worse of the lot.

TIGER: What joke is this, Otto?

OTTO: No joke, Tiger. All the women in the village threaten to wash me down with licks and stop buying in the shop, if I give you-all any more credit for drink. Only cash.

TIGER: What the hell is this! You hear that, Singh?

SINGH: Yes! It look like the women want some controlling!

MAN ONE [angrily]: Man Otto, stop making joke and bring a bottle!

OTTO: Let me see the colour of your money. Only cash customers, please. And make haste, I closing down just now…

MAN ONE: The women must of gone out of their heads!

MAN TWO: Is a long time they ain't get a good beating, if you ask me. They want some reminders of who is the boss, eh Tiger?

TIGER: Is who put them up to this, I wonder?

MAN TWO: I hear was your wife, Urmilla, who was the ring-leader!

TIGER: Eh-eh? Just let me get home! I will teach she a lesson she never forget!

MAN ONE: Me too, as soon as I reach I going to beat my wife like a snake!

MAN TWO: There will be weeping and wailing and gnashing of teeth in Five Rivers tonight!

A little later. Shrieks and screams come from all corners of the village…

WOMAN ONE: Oh God! Murder! Oh!

WOMAN TWO: Help! Police! Have mercy!

In TIGER's *and* URMILLA's *home,* BABOLAL *comes home to a strange scene.* TIGER *is thumping the table with a stick and* URMILLA *is screaming…*

TIGER: Take that, and that!

URMILLA [screaming]: Oh Lord, Tiger! Have mercy! I won't do it again, I swear!

TIGER: You had enough, you had enough?

URMILLA: Have mercy! Oh Lord!

[*They see* BABOLAL *and try hard to stifle their laughter…*]

96

BABOLAL: Like everybody gone crazy in Five Rivers tonight! Urmilla bawling like cow, and you hitting the table with a stick.

TIGER [*gasping*]: Oh, I never laugh so much for a long time… Tell him, Urmilla.

URMILLA: I can't stop laughing! …Tiger have to pretend he beating me, else all the other women would get suspicious.

TIGER: You lucky I got a sense of humour and see the funny side, and accept that you do it for my sake… It take some guts to do what you did… But stop laughing now, you lucky it wasn't a real beating.

URMILLA [*instantly docile*]: Yes Tiger. Tomorrow please God, I will tell Otto we change our minds.

BABOLAL: I don't know what you-all talking, but I hungry.

URMILLA: Your food hotting in the kitchen, Baboo. Go on, I will come just now and tell you what happen.

[BABOLAL *goes.*]

TIGER: The big question is a drink right now… I wonder if Soylo got an end hanging around… That remind me! You pack up my books like I asked you to?

URMILLA: Yes. Look them in that cardboard box in the corner.

TIGER: Good… I going to see Soylo.

URMILLA: So late? You got to climb that steep hill in the dark.

TIGER: Is moonlight… I want to have a little chat with him…

Later, outside SOYLO's *house,* TIGER, *panting from the effort of carrying the box of books, is taking a few deep breaths to catch his wind…*

TIGER [*shouts*]: Soy! You home?

SOYLO [*coming out*]: Who that?

TIGER: Me. Tiger.

SOYLO: Ah! You come to look for a drink, eh? I hear what happen in the village. Sit down on the step, you might be in luck… [*He goes into the house and reappears with a bottle.*] …We got to drink from the bottle though… Here.

TIGER [*taking a swig*]: Ah… thanks, Soy. First for the day… I bring a present for you. My books.

SOYLO: Books! That's what you got in that box?

TIGER: Yes. I don't want them any more. I done with all that.

SOYLO: A man don't done with books, Tiger. You should know that. People like you and me can't live without them.

97

TIGER: You got any?

SOYLO: No.

TIGER: And you still alive! ...I wanted to throw them on the cane-piece today and burn them, then I thought of you.

SOYLO: I old, Tiger, but you still a young man, learning.

TIGER [*taking a swig*]: Them books ain't learn me a damn thing. Is experience what teach you... I going to be like everybody else, and just live.

SOYLO [*taking a swig*]: You want to end up like me, living in a hut in the bush like a hermit?

TIGER: I don't care. In a couple of days I going home to Barataria.

SOYLO: You-all reaping tomorrow?

TIGER: Yes. Mr. Robinson say he want every man on the job, so we might finish in the evening... Why you don't come? I will fix the pay-sheets and give you extra time.

SOYLO: I had enough to do with cane, boy. All over this island I work on estates, and it never get me anywhere. Cane have too many connections with our people... Go on, have another drink. I got a next bottle.

TIGER: I don't want to drink too much. We making an early start in the fields tomorrow.

SOYLO: Ah, come on, man! You will sweat it out in the hot sun cutting all that cane...

The next day in the canefields. The sound of rumbling carts, lowing oxen, crack of whips, indistinct shouts...

BABOLAL: Hurry up! Work quick! Mr. Robinson say a bonus for the carts what carry the most loads!

MAN ONE: The women loading up too slow, Babolal...

BABOLAL: Tell Tiger to come over here, I want him...

MAN TWO [*driving a cart*]: Hi, mule, hi! You going too damn slow...

SINGH: You just drive your cart and leave me to cut cane, right?

MAN ONE: Tiger! Your father want to see you!

[MR. ROBINSON *comes over to* BABOLAL...]

ROBINSON: Babolal!

BABOLAL: Sir, Mr. Robinson!

ROBINSON: You've got too many men concentrated in the south field. Shift some of them. And the loading is too slow on the west side. Send four more carts over there.

BABOLAL: Right away, sir!

ROBINSON: What do you think of the weather? I don't like those ugly black clouds coming over the hills.

BABOLAL: Those only 'passing' clouds, sir.

ROBINSON: I hope so... How many loads so far on this side?

BABOLAL: Ten gone and two more to go, sir.

ROBINSON: Good. Keep moving. Don't slacken the pace. Let the men eat at work if they have to...

Back at TIGER's *and* URMILLA's *house,* BERTA *is helping* URMILLA *to pack...*

URMILLA: There, Berta... I too glad I had you to help me pack, otherwise I wouldn't of had time to cook.

BERTA: I going to miss you too bad when you go, Urmilla. The both of we was coming good friends.

URMILLA: You will soon have a baby to keep you company...

BERTA: The thing is, I don't know if is Otto or Singh!

URMILLA: You better watch out! If it don't have flat nose and chinky eyes, Otto will give you your share of the beating what you escape the other night...

Next morning. TIGER *is loading up the donkey cart...*

TIGER [*calling*]: Anything more, Urmilla?

URMILLA [*from the house*]: Just some pots and pans what I use to make breakfast. I bringing them now...

TIGER: Well, make haste! We late already, and I wanted to leave bright and early as the cock crow!

URMILLA [*coming*]: Well, if you didn't stay so long in the shop last night getting drunk with your friends, you would of got up earlier.

TIGER: Come, do be quick... We say goodbye to everybody already, so we don't have to linger. And Babolal waiting down by the track...

On their way out of the village, overlooking it, URMILLA *calls for the cart to stop...*

URMILLA: Hold up here by the mango tree, Baboo. Let we take a last look… This is just by where we stop when we was coming… You remember, Tiger?

TIGER: Yes… It seems like a long time ago… I learn a lot about life down in that valley…

URMILLA: Well, we not leaving empty-handed, praise the lord. I save up on the house-keeping money… and if you didn't drink so much, we would of had even more…

[*There are indistinct shouts from the distance…*]

URMILLA: …You hearing somebody call?

TIGER: I think so… Keep quiet and listen…

SOYLO [*calling from a little nearer*]: Ayee! Tiger-r-r! Wait a minute!

BABOLAL: It look like Soylo coming over there…

[SOYLO *comes up, breathless. He has the box of books.*]

SOYLO: I was calling. You didn't hear?

TIGER: The wind against you, man.

SOYLO: I just had this box for you… a present to take back.

TIGER: That look like my box of books, man!

SOYLO: You might need them, Tiger. You never know, a time might come when you regret you didn't have them… When you get out of Five Rivers, you got the whole world in front of you…

TIGER: But I give them to you, Soy. I can't take them back?

SOYLO: Well… I lending them to you, to look after for me. They will only get dust and mildew in my old hut.

URMILLA [*coaxing*]: Take them, Tiger. You know you like a fish out of water when you haven't got books… You would be miserable.

TIGER [*hesitant*]: Well…

BABOLAL [*grousily*]: Ah, put them in the cart, Soylo. Tiger always to-and-froing, as if he can't make up his mind. He must well be glad to have them back… Hi, donkey, hi!

[*The cart starts to move off…*]

TIGER: What you know about books, Babolal? If it wasn't for me…

URMILLA: Lord, don't start arguing again. We come arguing, and we leaving with an argument. Tiger, you go on and on…

THE END

HOME SWEET INDIA

Characters

JOHNNY: A middle-aged, hard-drinking jeweller
MARY: Johnny's long-suffering wife
JULIA: His daughter, who is looking for independence
JEAN: A flirtatious woman, a customer in Johnny's shop
GOVIND: Julia's boyfriend, a minor civil servant
DR. ROY WILKINS: An English doctor working in Trinidad
TAJ: Johnny's young shop assistant
LALLA: The leader of the return to India committee
GOPAUL: A prosperous business man
RADIO ANNOUNCER
NEWSPAPER VENDOR

Woodford Square, Port of Spain.
There are sounds of an animated public meeting. JOHNNY, LALLA *and*
GOPAUL *are on the platform.*

JOHNNY: Listen Lalla, I think we had enough speech. Is time for
some action. The crowd like it getting restless.

LALLA: All right, Johnny. I will just do a little summing-up... The
loud-speaker all right, Gopaul?

GOPAUL: Johnny better have a look at it... if he sober enough.

JOHNNY: You should be a scientist like me, Gopaul, and learn about
these elementary things. Let me see... [*He blows into the micro-
phone, and then speaks, forgetting to switch off.*] Testing, testing,
one, two, three... it all right, Gopaul. And I only had a nip of rum
this morning, you call that drinking? [*His voice booms over the
speaker and the crowd roars with laughter.*]

LALLA: Switch the damn thing off! That all the sense you have?

GOPAUL: And then he say he wasn't drinking!

LALLA: You got the National Anthem ready, Johnny?

JOHNNY: It right here in my hand.

GOPAUL: Best watch that record before you break it!

LALLA: Now is no time to make jokes, man... Hand me the mike.

[*The crowd cheers as* LALLA *prepares to speak.*]

[*On mike*] Thank you, thank you! Now countrymen, everybody
got their placards and signs?

[*Affirmative cries from the crowd*]

Good. Hold them up high, so people who passing through
Woodford Square could see... We got to convince the Government that we not making joke when we say we want to go back
to India. Remember they bring we here to work in the canefields
as indentured labourers, and now that the Mother Country have
independence, we have a right to make the Government send
we back! This morning we going to march round the Red
House, and then we going to the Governor House round the
savannah. I don't want no trouble with the police. March in
peace, keep in line and don't jam up the traffic. Mr. Johnny and
Mr. Gopaul, my two assistants, will lead you-all... [*Off mike,
now*] Put the record on now, Johnny.

103

JOHNNY: I trying… like the needle stick… Is the first time this ever happen, and I just overhaul the record player before bringing it… Must of been my stupid wife Mary or daughter Julia interfering with it.

GOPAUL: Big inventor like you can't fix it?

JOHNNY: Ah… it all right now…

[*The strains of the Indian National Anthem goes over the speaker… The crowd begins to sing and march off.*]

A little later at JOHNNY'*s Jewellery Shop.*

JEAN: But Taj! I left that wristwatch with Mr. Johnny since last week, and he promise to repair it same day.

TAJ: He got about fifteen wristwatch on the workbench here, and all of them in pieces, mix up with all kinds of stupidness what he say he inventing.

JEAN: Well look for mine. Is a gold one, twenty-jewel.

TAJ: Jean, you better come back later when Johnny come… Why you didn't give it to me personally?

JEAN: You wasn't in the shop when I bring it.

TAJ: I would of done a private job, you mightn't of even had to pay… [*Suggestive*] …in money, I mean.

JEAN [*giggling*]: You too fast, Taj!

TAJ: I can't find it anywhere.

JEAN: Look in them little envelopes what he keep under the counter.

TAJ [*searching*]: Ah! Fifteen Rose Hill… that's your address?

JEAN: Yes!

TAJ: You lucky… let me set it for you…

JEAN: I hope it don't give me any more trouble. I keep bringing it back all the time. It must of cost me more repairing it than what I pay Mr. Johnny for it in the first place.

TAJ: There… it sound as if it ticking all right.

JEAN: I hope it tocking, too! How much?

TAJ: As it's you, Jean, I mightn't charge you… if I could pay a little visit up Rose Hill?

JEAN: You got to do better than that, Taj! How much is that brooch in the glass case?

TAJ: That one? Ten dollars.

JEAN: Ten dollars!

TAJ: It make of cultured pearls... You like it? You think it worth a little visit?

JEAN [*giggling*]: But Taj, you really good for yourself, yes! You don't know I is a married woman with a child?

TAJ: All the sweeter!

JEAN: Is a nice brooch... Take it out, let me try it on.

[*She is pinning on the brooch when* JOHNNY *comes in.*]

JOHNNY: You still here boy? I thought I fire you yesterday.

JEAN: Mr. Johnny! You can't make this brooch any cheaper for me?

JOHNNY: It cheap enough for seven dollars.

JEAN: Seven? Taj just tell me...

TAJ [*interrupting quickly*]: Leave it for when you passing again, Jean.

JEAN: Oh... all right. I got to get to the market now, in all this.

JOHNNY: See how much empty bottles it have there, boy. I thirsty after all that marching.

TAJ: That's just a waste of time... I know a lot of Indians who don't want to go back.

JOHNNY: What you know about politics?

TAJ: It say so in the papers. It have some old people who want to go, but young people like me, what we got in India?

JOHNNY: What you got in Trinidad?

TAJ: I born here.

JOHNNY [*derisive*]: You don't even know! You come from an orphanage in British Guiana, and if you don't look sharp, I send you back there to plant rice in the mud! Go on, count the bottles.

TAJ: It only have nine. You need another one for a full free bottle.

JOHNNY: Tell the rumshop you owe them one. And come back quick. Don't think I don't know you does have a few drinks on the quiet. I just waiting to catch you red-handed and bam! I will fire you.

TAJ [*grumbling*]: The amount of times you fire me, I should of burn down already!

JOHNNY: Don't give me no backchat... and when you come back, go and get my lunch... Tell Mrs. Johnny to send a fresh pepper with the food...

Meanwhile at JOHNNY's *house,* MARY, *his wife, and his daughter,* JULIA, *are at home.* JULIA *comes from the kitchen to* MARY, *who is sitting in a rocking chair reading the newspapers.*

JULIA: Ma, you still reading the papers?

MARY: Look at this photo, Julia. A English doctor come to open up practice in Trinidad.

JULIA: You don't give up do you? You keep inviting these men here, and I keep insulting them.

MARY: I got to get a husband for you, girl… you should of married some professional who got money like a barrister or a doctor.

JULIA: You does talk sometimes like the Indians living in the countryside, as if you don't know them days finish. You think I want to get married under a bamboo tent?

MARY: You better don't let your father hear you talking like that.

JULIA: The both of you always treating me like a child… Anyway, I finish boiling the split-peas. You coming to chunkay the dhal?

MARY [*getting up, closing the paper*]: All right… [*She follows* JULIA *to the kitchen, still talking.*] I think I will try to get that doctor to come for dinner soon… Don't mind he white.

JULIA [*sarcastic*]: I thought Indian should married Indian? One minute you say one thing, and the next minute you contradict yourself.

MARY: Chop the onions for me… I was looking for an Indian, but I don't see any. [MARY *opens tins and gets spices together and begins to grind them in a stone bowl.*]

JULIA [*pause*]: Ma, I finish with commercial lessons. I going to look for a job.

MARY: A job! You know your father don't like you taking shorthand and typing, much more a job!

JULIA: What's the use of going to school then?

MARY: Put the onion in the frying pan.

JULIA: Another thing I want to tell you… this talk about going back to India… I hope you-all not including me in that. I don't know nothing about India except what I learn in school when I was small.

MARY: I don't know what your father deciding, girl. He went out early to some meeting in Woodford Square.

JULIA: You know he is like a stranger to me, so I telling you so you could tell him…

MARY: There, the dhal finish.

JULIA: Just in time, I hear Taj coming.

MARY [*sternly as* TAJ *comes in*]: Taj! You know Mr. Johnny doesn't like you to use the front door.

TAJ: I was late, M's Mary, that's why... He say don't forget to put in a fresh pepper.

MARY: I suppose he must be drinking... Go in the yard and pick one for me.

[TAJ *moves off*, JULIA *following him...*]

JULIA [*low voice*]: Taj! You give Govind the message?

TAJ: Yes... He say to meet him in the square after lunch.

JULIA: Good. Thanks...

Later, in the square.

GOVIND: Julia! I though you wasn't coming again.

JULIA: So much trouble to get out of that house... Where you going, who you going to see, what time you coming back... I tired of it, Govind.

GOVIND: Come, let's sit under the poui tree on that bench. [*They move to the bench and sit.*]

JULIA: I can't stay too long... I hope nobody see us.

GOVIND: You only just got here, Julia, and you talking about going back already.

JULIA: Don't quarrel.

GOVIND: And not only that. We got to hide every time.

JULIA: You think I like it?

GOVIND: Things can't go on like this. The only place we can make love in is in the back seat of the theatre, or find some lonely spot in the botanical gardens.

JULIA: Pa like he want to go to India, Govind... I wish it really happen.

GOVIND: He wouldn't leave you behind!

JULIA: I going to tell him flat I not going.

GOVIND: You're only saying that... How many times already you promise to make them realise you not a little girl?

JULIA: Pa not easy to talk to... He and me never have much to say to each other... Yet I like him, you know.... but as if he live in one world and I in another.

GOVIND: You could have it out with Mary.

JULIA: As for her! She still trying to married me off, reading the papers every day, looking for some lawyer or doctor.

GOVIND: Maybe she right. Maybe I only a clerk in the civil service, and my father does drive a truck to make a living...

JULIA: You think I care about that?

GOVIND: What hurts me is this big pride your family have, and look at Johnny, living in a state of drunkenness. People find him lying on the pavement and have to carry him home.

JULIA [*defensively*]: He not always drunk you know.

GOVIND: Tell me when he sober! Everybody in Port of Spain know him so well.

JULIA: He still my father!

GOVIND: Who quarrelling now?

JULIA: You start it.

GOVIND: Well, I can't blame them if they want to marry you to a man with wealth and position... Maybe I should get white skin and go away and study law or medicine.

JULIA: You still going on and on.

GOVIND [*as if to himself*]: What beats me is how your mother does it... gets on the phone, I suppose, and calls some friend who knows somebody who knows the eligible bachelor of the moment... She really brass face, yes!

JULIA [*coldly*]: You finish?

GOVIND: I just start...

JULIA [*getting up*]: Well, *I* finish. Goodbye. [*She walks away quickly.*]

GOVIND: Julia! Wait! I'm sorry, I didn't... When will I see you?

The next day in JOHNNY's *bedroom.*

JOHNNY [*yawning and muttering to himself*]: I wonder where that blasted Mary hide the rum this time? One day I going to give she one clout behind she head and make she basodee... [*Aloud*] Mary!

[JULIA *comes in.*]

JULIA: What you want, Pa?

JOHNNY: I ain't call you. Where your mother?

JULIA: Her hands in the flour, she can't come now.

JOHNNY: You know which part she hide my rum? I had a little nip on the ground here by the bed.

JULIA: First thing in the morning, Pa! You know what the doctor say.

JOHNNY: Never mind no damn doctor. I will live longer than that rogue... The *Guardian* come yet?

JULIA: Ma was looking at it.

JOHNNY: Go and bring it. I tired tell both of you nobody must read the papers before me.

[JULIA *goes out and* JOHNNY *gets up and moves to search for the rum.*]

JOHNNY: Aha! I thought so. Behind the dressing-table... [*He chuckles.*] She so foolish, she always hide it in the same place!... [*He uncorks the bottle and takes a swig.*] ...A-ah! Nothing like a shot to open your eyes in the morning.

[JULIA *returns with the newspaper.*]

JULIA: Here it is.

JOHNNY: Any news about the march yesterday?

JULIA: I didn't read it.

JOHNNY: And the ship... nothing? It should be on the front page.

JULIA: What ship?

JOHNNY: The ship what coming to take we back to India. Don't play as if you don't know... Is back to India for every manjack... [*He crumbles the paper in disgust.*] Not a damn thing on the front page! They should burn the *Guardian*.

MARY [*from the kitchen*]: Julia!

JULIA: Coming Ma.

[JULIA *leaves to join* MARY *in the kitchen.*]

MARY: The flour finish kneading. Make some sardah roti whilst I do the bul-jol.

JULIA: Ma, you tell Pa about the job?

MARY: I ain't get a chance.

JULIA: Well I not taking any more stupid commercial lessons... Is a good job, in the public library.

MARY: Your father head only full of this India business... I don't want to aggravate him.

JULIA: How Pa could want us to leave everything we got in Trinidad and go to India to live? He must be crack in the head.

[JOHNNY *hears this as he comes in.*]

JOHNNY: Crack in the head eh? We will see who crack in the head, young lady, when the time come.

JULIA [*gasping*]: Oh!

MARY [*calling*]: Taj! Hurry up in the W.C. …Mr. Johnny waiting.

JOHNNY [*boisterous*]: That vagabond should be the one waiting. Is not enough we give him a room in the back here to live, he want to rule the roost, too! [*Shouting*] Taj! You fired!

MARY: Don't fire him yet, Johnny. I want him to go to the market for a fresh piece of beef.

JOHNNY: All right then. But tomorrow!…

> [JOHNNY *sits down to breakfast. There is a nervous silence as he begins to eat.*]

JOHNNY [*with his mouth full*]: Who make these roti? It want more salt… Why you didn't get an avocado, woman, you know I like it with the bul-jol… [*There is more silence as he eats.*] Like everybody lose their tongues this morning!

JULIA: Pa

JOHNNY: Don't say nothing! As for you, I don't know why your mother don't married you off! The chair you sitting on not good enough, eh? You prefer a bench in Woodford Square?

JULIA: What…

JOHNNY: Don't interrupt! You think Johnny crack in the head, eh? Johnny going to surprise you, and surprise the world, one of these days… Just let me set my hand on gravity with my invention… What happen to you, Mary? Cat cut out your tongue?… You afraid to answer eh? You letting this daughter of yours traipse all over town scandalising my name… You better lock she up in the house until we ready to go.

MARY [*in a burst*]: Why you don't leave the poor girl alone? Who talking? You or Mr. Rum? You got a house in India? You got a job over there?

JOHNNY: Don't backchat me. What I say is Law. And I say we going back where our roots come from, as soon as the government send the ship.

MARY: You think the government have time to bother with all those stupid people marching about and making speech in the square?

JOHNNY: You don't know nothing about politics, woman. What's the time?

MARY: You got a wristwatch on your hand.

JOHNNY: It not carrying right time.

110

MARY: Is time to go and open the shop… Don't forget to leave some money to run the house.

JOHNNY [*pushes his chair back and gets up. He puts a dollar on the table*]: Here. Look a dollar. I suppose I better go, before that blooming boy rob me. He think I don't know he take in private jobs, but just let me catch him and I fire him like a bullet.

[*He leaves the house.*]

JULIA [*with a short ironic laugh*]: What sort of life is this we leading? I don't know if to laugh or cry.

MARY: You should know what your father like by now.

JULIA: We can't go on like this… You think he serious about India?

MARY: Who could tell with him? We just got to wait and see.

JULIA: What going to happen to me? You and Pa not even give me a chance to breathe. Now he want to lock me up in the house like a prisoner.

MARY [*sighing*]: We should have married you off when you was small.

JULIA: Don't keep on with that song, Ma.

MARY: All the same, I manage to get Dr. Wilkins to come for dinner this evening… you remember, the young Englishman who was in the papers.

JULIA: I will insult him, I warning you!

MARY: You heard what your father say. You want to be locked in the house?

JULIA: I don't care. I going to run away and live by myself somewhere… I can't bear this no more.

MARY: You must put on a new sari… dress up pretty. You could use lipstick… and watch your manners. Don't talk no bad English … Is all for your own good, Julia. One day you going to thank me for it…

JOHNNY's *shop.* TAJ *is beating out a piece of gold.* JOHNNY *is working on a contraption.*

JOHNNY [*muttering to himself*]: This spinwheel here… just slip this little shaft so… u'mm [*Loud now*] Boy, don't hammer so loud…

[TAJ *ignores him,* JOHNNY *continues to mutter.*]

Once I give it a spin, it shouldn't stop, it should go on spinning forever, as long as the earth spin… [*Loudly*] I say stop pounding, boy!

[TAJ *stops this time. In a rage* JOHNNY *scatters the small instruments and parts he has been working with.*]

…This blasted thing! A man can't concentrate. Boy, you fired.

TAJ [*resuming hammering*]: What for this time?

JOHNNY: Distracting me from my work.

TAJ: You call that work? Playing inventor? If it wasn't for me, the shop gone bankrupt long time!

JOHNNY: Don't display your ignorance, boy. You know anything about science?

TAJ: What it is you trying to do?

JOHNNY: Come, come over here, let me teach you…

[TAJ *moves close.*]

Now. You know what gravity is? You remember when you was in school and the teacher tell you about that fellar Newton, how he sit down under a mango tree and a mango fall, and how he invent Gravity?

TAJ: He didn't invent it. It was there all the time.

JOHNNY: Aha! And it still there today! Now boy, that is a force that does pull things down, right? Suppose now you could harness that force and make it pull things sideways, and forwards and backwards? Eh? You got enough brains to understand what I talking about? You won't need no engine, or gasolene, or no atom power, or nothing.

TAJ: And that little contraption you got there could do all that?

JOHNNY: This is just a model.

TAJ: Make it work. Let me see.

JOHNNY: That's what I trying to do, you damn fool! But you keeping so much noise in the shop I can't concentrate.

TAJ: You want me to beat out that sheet of gold, don't you? I mean, if both of we play Inventor, no work get done in the shop.

JOHNNY: You fired!

TAJ: Best watch out I don't take you serious one day!

JOHNNY: I don't doubt. You must of t'ief and swindle me enough to open up you own business. Just let me catch you at it, that's all…

[JEAN *comes into the shop.*]

JEAN [*plaintively*]: Mr. Johnny! The wristwatch stop again!

JOHNNY: What wristwatch?

JEAN: The same one; you think I have two? It only work for about one hour yesterday.

TAJ [*sarcastically*]: Maybe you should harness it with Gravity.

JOHNNY: I thought I fire you? You still here?

JEAN: Why you don't give me a new one, Mr. Johnny, and keep this stupid one?

JOHNNY: Take it off and let me see

[JEAN *gives it to him.*]

...h'mm... [*He winds it.*] Maybe you allergic to watches.

JEAN [*puzzled*]: Alagic?

JOHNNY: Yes. It have some people like that; watches don't agree with them.

JEAN: But eh-eh! You mean I got to see a doctor?

JOHNNY: Leave it with me. I'll take a look when I time. Come back next week.

JEAN: I can't wait so long.

JOHNNY: Here, Taj, see what you could do with it. I got to go out to a meeting.

TAJ: What time you coming back?

JOHNNY: Unexpected, to see if I catch you transacting any private business... and then I won't only fire you, but I let the police lock you up in jail and throw away the key...

LALLA'*s house.* LALLA *and* GOPAUL *are waiting for* JOHNNY *who is late.*

LALLA: Ah, Johnny. We said we was to meet at eleven o'clock, and is almost half past now.

JOHNNY: I got a lot of work in the shop, Lalla.

GOPAUL: You must of stopped off in the rumshop... I could smell your breath.

LALLA: Alright, Gopaul, the both of you always arguing.

GOPAUL: Well, I don't think Johnny treating this matter serious at all. I mean, at least he could have waited until after the meeting to start drinking.

JOHNNY [*scoffing*]: Next thing, you want to tell me when to go to sleep and when to get up.

113

LALLA [*sharply*]: Enough! Sit down, Johnny. I was just telling Gopaul about developments… We had a committee meeting last night… All over the island we got the people on our side and the government got to do something.

JOHNNY: Is about time too. I don't know about you-all, but I start packing.

GOPAUL: You talking as if you going to spend the weekend in San Fernando. India not a few miles away you know.

JOHNNY: You telling me where India is, my mother country?

GOPAUL: I only know it got a lot of people like you in Trinidad who only have Christian names, who don't bother to observe our customs and religion or anything. And always pretending to be in the front when the Indians have any trouble.

JOHNNY: You describe yourself exactly. That big store you have down Frederick Street, and all that taxi business you running… I want to see you leave all that and return to Mother India… Lalla, we got to watch this man. Ten to one, when the time come, he back out and say he rather stay in Trinidad.

LALLA: Anybody who want to remain better make up their minds. Because we going to take some drastic steps… The government moving too slow, and the committee decide to take action.

JOHNNY: What action?

LALLA [*dramatically*]: We going to threaten MASS SUICIDE unless they send we back.

JOHNNY: Mass suicide! You mean everybody?

LALLA: All those Indians who believe in what we doing.

GOPAUL: That really is a drastic step, Lalla.

JOHNNY [*sneering*]: What happen, Gopaul, you frighten already?

GOPAUL: What I mean is, how we going to do that?

LALLA: That's the problem the committee gave us to solve. Is no use just threatening, we got to plan it out in detail as if it going to happen in truth, else the government would feel we only making grand-charge.

GOPAUL: But suppose it happen for real?

JOHNNY: Well, suppose it happen? You ready to run, eh Gopaul? Life too sweet, eh?

GOPAUL: How about you? I suppose you going to be the first man to cut your throat?

LALLA: That's not how it going to be done. In the first place, we have

114

to give the government an ultimatum. How long you think, Johnny?

JOHNNY: That up to the committee, ain't it?

LALLA: Yes, but we got to make suggestions… About a week?

JOHNNY: So long!

GOPAUL [*quickly*]: That ain't long. You know how slow the government work… I would say a month or more, myself. You got to give people a chance to contemplate dying of a sudden.

JOHNNY: How much time you want, Gopaul, a year?

GOPAUL: Let's just suppose the government don't do anything.

LALLA: Don't forget the Indians make up more than one third of the population. They bound to pay attention.

GOPAUL: Yes, but how much of that third go be prepared to hang themselves, or whatever?

JOHNNY: I could see that of the three of we here, one dropping out already.

LALLA: Is nothing to joke about, Johnny. Every man got to make his own decision.

JOHNNY: I agree with you, Lalla. But if Gopaul not patriotic to the cause he better say so now, and drop out. Is no use he try to fool anybody.

GOPAUL: Listen, I am a business man. I got a lot of money invest in Trinidad. And besides, I got a family of ten children. Johnny only got one child – and not even a boy. He don't have no worries.

LALLA: I didn't get the two of you here to discuss your personal life. I want some suggestions… I think a week good enough. The next thing is the question of suicide, how to do it and where.

JOHNNY: We could throw pitchoil on everybody and strike a match. In front the Red House, in Woodford Square… What you say, Gopaul?

GOPAUL [*shuddering*]: I rather shoot myself.

JOHNNY: It don't matter how you dead. Once you dead, you dead.

LALLA: We must think of something that have *dignity* in it. I thought we could just stop breathing.

JOHNNY: That sound too peaceful. We must draw attention to the sacrifice we making… How about if we all march to St. Peter's Bay and throw weself in the sea, singing *Jana-Gana-Mana*? You could swim, Lalla?

LALLA: No.

JOHNNY: Well then!

LALLA: That might work… but I want some more ideas, just for the committee to select from.

JOHNNY: Well look. How about if I invent a big explosion, and blow up everybody in Woodford Square? That would make plenty noise!

LALLA: That might be too dangerous.

JOHNNY: Not if I invent it. I could make a timing device so it go off at the right time… And we could still sing the National Anthem.

LALLA: I like the part of the singing, anyway. Whatever we do, I think we should be singing when it happen… You got any ideas, Gopaul?

GOPAUL [*clearing his throat nervously*]: You think it would really reach a stage where we have to do something like that?

LALLA: We got to be prepared to face our destiny.

GOPAUL: My brain not working good at the moment… I will see if I could think up something good later.

JOHNNY: You do that, Gopaul. Go home and say your prayers, you might get an inspiration.

GOPAUL: At least I could do that, but what you would do when you go home. Help Mary look for a husband for Miss Julia?

JOHNNY [*blustering*]: What you talking about?

GOPAUL [*sneering*]: The whole of Port of Spain talking about it. It ain't no secret that your wife Mary trying desperately to married off your daughter. You coming here with big talk and you can't even manage your own responsibilities in your own house…

At JOHNNY's *house.* MARY *and* JULIA *are getting ready to receive their guest.*

MARY: You better put on the blue sari, you look good in that.

JULIA: I don't care how I look.

MARY: And some lipstick, and some rouge… but don't forget to wipe it off before your father come home.

JULIA: Ma, I warning you. This is the last time. Is only because you invite this man already and I don't want to shame you… You promise?

MARY: Yes, yes… What's the time? Five o'clock? I better put the rice on the fire… Look that chair still have dust on it. [*Calls*] Taj!

TAJ [*coming from the kitchen*]: Yes M's Mary?

MARY: You didn't polish the furniture good. Look at the chair, it still dusty.

TAJ [*grumbling*]: I know to polish silver and gold, not no old chair and table.

MARY: I better get in the kitchen... Julia, don't waste time. You should be dress and waiting when the doctor comes...

[MARY *goes.*]

JULIA [*in a low voice*]: Taj! You didn't see Govind today?

TAJ: Yes, he pass round by the shop.

JULIA: Only now you telling me?

TAJ: I didn't get a chance before.

JULIA: He give you any message?

TAJ: He say he got to see you this evening.

JULIA: But Ma invite this man to dinner.

TAJ: He say that's why. He say by hook or by crook he going to pass in front the house about six o'clock and whistle. And if you don't go out, he say he finish.

JULIA: But Taj, you know I like a prisoner here! And this stupid whiteman coming. What I going to do?

TAJ: I have a scheme. I don't know if it will work, but when Govind whistle... [*He whispers something in her ear.*]

A little later, the door bell rings. JULIA *opens the door to* DR. WILKINS. *He knows what* MARY *is up to through the friend who extended the invitation.*

WILKINS: Good evening. Is this where Mr. Johnny lives?

JULIA: Yes.

WILKINS: Is Mrs. Johnny in?

JULIA: Yes.

WILKINS: I believe she is expecting me?

JULIA [*calling*]: Ma, you expecting a visitor?

MARY [*coming up*]: You know that! Come in, Dr. Wilkins, come in and sit down...

JULIA [*shutting the door*]: Not that chair by the window, that's mine.

WILKINS: Oh... sorry. Is this one all right?

MARY: Any chair, Doctor... This is my daughter, Julia. She very good at shorthand and typing...

JULIA: Oh Ma!

WILKINS: Er... I thought Mr. Sharma might have been here?

MARY: He phone to say he couldn't make it, as something unexpected turn up suddenly... But Sharma is no stranger like you; he could always come... Julia, what about a drink for the Doctor?

JULIA: You forget Taj here?

MARY: Oh yes. I will send him in with something right away... Just excuse me for a minute, Doctor. Julia, why you don't put some music on the gramophone?

[MARY *goes to the kitchen...* JULIA *goes to the record player.*]

JULIA [*abruptly*]: What you like to hear?

WILKINS: I love the steel band music... [*After a pause*] I've got a confession to make... I can't pretend any longer.

JULIA: Pretend what?

WILKINS: That I don't know what all this is about... It isn't fair to you. You see, Sharma's a good friend of mine. We met when he was in England.

JULIA: I don't understand?

WILKINS: I know how desperate your parents are to have you married... That's why I'm here, isn't it?

JULIA: Oh no!

WILKINS [*quickly*]: You've nothing to fear from me... I have no matrimonial intentions.

JULIA: Oh no! You mean... you just come here to humiliate and shame me?

WILKINS: Not at all. Perhaps I did think in the beginning that the situation might be amusing, but it's obvious to me that you're embarrassed... I'm sorry, Julia.

JULIA: You only come here to insult me!

WILKINS: If I wanted to do that, I wouldn't have told you... Now that we understand each other, perhaps we can be friends?

JULIA: I feel so ashamed!

WILKINS: Please don't be... It's got a funny side, don't you think, now we both know?

JULIA: I... I suppose so.

WILKINS: You're a lovely girl... Don't you want to marry?

JULIA: Of course! I've got a boy friend.

WILKINS: I'd be surprised if you hadn't. What's his name?

JULIA: Govind.

WILKINS: And your father and mother don't know, I presume… What're you going to do?

JULIA: That's what's worrying me.

WILKINS: Well, you can relax. I've no intentions of wooing you away from Govind. So please stop staring out into the street and let's chat… My name is Roy. If you use it I'll know you're not offended.

JULIA [with a dry laugh]: It's a big joke.

WILKINS: Then let's enjoy it… Here's Taj with the drinks.

[TAJ comes in with a tray of drinks.]

TAJ: Doctor, sir, what you like to have? We got gin, whisky, rum, sherry.

WILKINS: What'll you like, Julia? A sherry?

JULIA [at ease now]: I'll try a rum and coke, please Roy.

WILKINS: Rum and coke for the lady, Taj. And I'll have the same.

[TAJ pours the drinks.]

WILKINS: Let's drink to what we know, Julia, and keep it secret. That'll be fun.

JULIA: Okay, Roy… you could leave the drinks, Taj.

TAJ: Yes, Miss Julia.

TAJ puts the drinks on the table and returns to the kitchen, where MARY is preparing food.

MARY [in an anxious low voice]: They talking, Taj?

TAJ [excitedly]: Yes!

MARY: What about?

TAJ: I don't rightly know, but she calling him 'Roy' and he calling her 'Julia'. And they was saying something about a secret.

MARY: In truth? I must take a peep! [Moves to the door and looks] Yes! they laughing and drinking! It looks as if the doctor like she!

TAJ: Miss Julia has a rum and coke.

MARY: Maybe she might catch the white doctor… I hope so…

Back in the living room with JULIA and WILKINS.

JULIA: …and when Govind pass and whistle, Taj going to call him round by the back entrance, and I going to make an excuse and try and see him.

WILKINS: So that's why you keep sitting by the window… Can't you ask him in?

JULIA: Lord, he's never been in this house.

WILKINS: Well, it's about time, don't you think… Let's say he's my friend.

JULIA: I think that's him coming down the road now!

[*There is a distant whistle, repeated once or twice.*]

WILKINS: Go on Julia, be brave! Open the door!

[JULIA *opens the door and calls out low and urgently.*]

JULIA: Govind! Come! Come inside!

GOVIND [*approaching*]: You mean in the house?

JULIA: Yes, it's alright.

GOVIND: You sure?

JULIA: Yes, come on!

[GOVIND *enters and she shuts the door.*]

WILKINS [*loud and hearty*]: Govind, my good friend! How lucky you were passing by.

JULIA: Listen Govind, I better explain quickly what happening.

[TAJ *comes in. He is astonished to see* GOVIND *in the house.*]

TAJ: Govind! What you doing here?

JULIA: Just tell Ma a friend of Dr. Wilkins is here, Taj. Go on!

TAJ [*astonished*]: A friend… All right, all right. [*Goes*]

JULIA [*whispers*]: Is Roy's idea, Govind!

GOVIND: But I…

[MARY *comes in.*]

JULIA: Ma, this is a good friend of Dr. Wilkins… This is my mother, Govind.

GOVIND: I'm happy to meet you, Mrs. Johnny.

MARY: You is a doctor too?

JULIA: Govind has a good Government job… Everybody can't be doctors and lawyers.

WILKINS: That's true. I was a Government official myself, before I came out to Trinidad.

MARY: You just in time to have some dinner with us, Mr. Govind.

GOVIND: You didn't expect me… I don't want to give you trouble.

MARY: We have plenty… I won't keep you all waiting long.

WILKINS: Have a drink, Govind.

GOVIND: If only you know how nervous I feeling!

JULIA: I'll pour you a rum and coke… It will steady your nerves!

WILKINS [as JULIA fixes a drink]: You two are in a spot, aren't you? You ought to have it out with them.

GOVIND: That's what I keep telling Julia… before Johnny takes her back to India.

WILKINS: I heard something about that. What started it?

GOVIND: It's the old generation. They want to return now that India's got independence.

JULIA: They will have to tie me and carry me on board that ship!

WILKINS: Are all the Indians on the island going?

GOVIND: Oh no. But it doesn't look as if Julia is going to have any choice.

[There is a sound of a taxi pulling up outside.]

WILKINS: Hello! Looks like we're having more company.

[They can hear JOHNNY arguing outside with the taxi driver about the fare.]

JOHNNY: A dollar just to drop a man around the corner? You damn rogue and vagabond.

JULIA [disconcerted]: Oh Lord, Pa back all ready! Ma wasn't expecting him till late!

GOVIND: And it sound if he well charge up too.

JULIA: I better get Ma quick!

[JOHNNY staggers in loudly singing the Indian National Anthem. He breaks off abruptly as he sees the visitors.]

JOHNNY: What the hell is this! A white man in my house!

[MARY and JULIA come rushing in.]

MARY: Now Johnny…

JOHNNY: That blasted taxi driver overcharge me.

MARY [coaxing]: Come and go to sleep, you must be tired.

121

JOHNNY: Sleep! What happen, I not good enough for your guests? Who is this white man, pray?

JULIA: This is Doctor Wil…

JOHNNY: Doctor eh? All the doctors in Trinidad is rogues. Especially the white ones. Who had the bold face to invite this man?

JULIA: Pa, why you don't go and lay down…

JOHNNY: Enough time for that, girl, when all of we commit *mass suicide* to show the government we mean business.

MARY: Doctor, please excuse him. As you can see, he had too much to drink and don't know what he saying.

JOHNNY: You up to your old tricks, Mary? Matchmaking for your daughter?

MARY [*calling*]: Taj! Come give me a hand to put Mr. Johnny in bed… [*Lower to the others*] Sometimes he does listen to Taj…

JOHNNY: You listen to *me*. I don't want no white man for my daughter. I don't care if he is the king of England. When she married she got to married to Indian like sheself… like this boy here. What you name? [*To* GOVIND] …As if I seen your face before.

GOVIND: Govind, Mr. Johnny.

JOHNNY: A good Indian name. They didn't give you no stupid Christian one when you were born.

[TAJ *comes.*]

MARY: Look Taj here, Johnny, let him help you… [*To* TAJ] Hold him on the other side, Taj.

JOHNNY [*flinging their hands off*]: Leave me alone! You think I can't walk by myself? Watch!

[*He staggers off to the bedroom singing.*]

JOHNNY [*singing in his bedroom*]: Jana-gana-mana… Glory to thee, ruler of our hearts and of India's destiny…

MARY: Come Taj, we better look after him… bringing shame and disgrace in the house…

[*They follow* JOHNNY *out.*]

JULIA: I'm sorry, Roy. Pa always drinks too much. The doctor say it going to kill him one day.

WILKINS: Don't apologise… I'll leave. It's the best thing.

JULIA: But Ma cook so much food!

WILKINS: And I'm hungry too… But this is a chance for you and Govind. He should stay.

GOVIND: It looks bad to let you go like this.

WILKINS: I'll only be in the way. There's some hope for you and Julia now, if you play it right… I'm glad I came, if it helped to get you together.

JULIA: If it wasn't for you, Roy, Govind might of never set foot in this house.

WILKINS: Well, I wish you the best of luck. You must come and see me some time, and let me know how things turn out…

Next day…

NEWSPAPER VENDOR [*shouting*]: Get your G-u-a-r-d-i-a-n here! Read about the Indians going to kill themselves… *Guardian*!

RADIO ANNOUNCER: The main item of the news this morning is the threat to the Government by a large body of the East Indian community to commit suicide unless the Government take action to send them back to India. An emergency meeting of the Legislative Council will be held at the Red House this morning to consider this latest dramatic move in the campaign…

SPEAKER AT THE RED HOUSE: Gentlemen, it would seem that we have been treating this matter lightly, and there may be great temptation to continue doing so with what appears to be an irrational threat. But we must proceed now as if this mass suicide may really happen, and I need not tell you what the repercussions will be, not only in this small island but around the world.

In JOHNNY's *shop. He is humming an Indian air to himself as he concentrates on making the suicide weapon.*

JOHNNY: Ah Boy, what keep you so long?

TAJ: Like you want me to get in trouble with the police?

JOHNNY: What happen?

TAJ: You don't know you can't buy gunpowder without a licence.

JOHNNY: You get it though?

TAJ: In the end, yes. Only when I mention your name… It wrap up in this package, and the shopkeeper say you got to be careful. Here.

JOHNNY [taking package]: Good.

TAJ: If you going to experiment with gunpowder, I getting out of the shop.

JOHNNY: This is no experiment, boy. I know what I doing.

TAJ: All the same, I rather go home and help Mrs. Johnny clean out or something… What you was trying to make, anyway?

JOHNNY: I am not trying. I *making* a bomb. I been working on the diagram for three days.

TAJ: You not satisfy *harvesting* Mr. Gravity, now you want to split Mr. Atom! You going to blow up the shop?

JOHNNY: This is for the patriots who challenge the Government. Just one explosion and bam! Everybody blow up in Woodford Square… You could do sums?

TAJ: Sure.

JOHNNY: Work this out for me. If it takes two ounces of powder to blow up one man, how much it take to blow up two-three hundred?

[Before TAJ can answer, the phone rings. He picks it up.]

TAJ [on phone]: This is Johnny's Jewels Limited… Yes, Mr. Lalla, just hold on… [To JOHNNY] Mr. Lalla want to talk to you.

JOHNNY: Tell him I'm busy on the bomb.

TAJ [on phone]: Mr. Johnny say he busy… yes… [To JOHNNY] He say it urgent.

JOHNNY: Oh, all right. Pass the phone… [On phone] Lalla? I just in the middle of my invention… What? A ship? You sure? But I start already… All right, I will come over right away… [He hangs up. To TAJ] It looks like the government getting a ship.

TAJ: A ship? What for?

JOHNNY: To send we back to India… [Grumbling to himself] It look like the rascals get to hear of my gunpowder plot…

[JEAN comes into the shop.]

JEAN: Mr. Johnny! I glad I catch you. This wristwatch…

JOHNNY: Not now girl. I got to go to an important meeting. Talk to Taj. [He goes.]

124

TAJ: Look how the man leave that gunpowder expose. I better put it in a tin or something.

JEAN: Taj, this stupid wristwatch still giving trouble. If it ain't working slow, it working fast.

TAJ: It look like we have to fix you up with a sun-dial.

JEAN: What's that.

[TAJ *gets one from under the counter.*]

TAJ: Here. Look at it. Is the oldest clock in the world.

JEAN: That old thing could tell time? It ain't even got engine!

TAJ: All you have to do is put it in the yard and this thing here make a shadow when the sun shine.

JEAN: H'mm. What happen when rain fall?

TAJ: When rain fall? You and me will be inside cuddling up and sheltering, Jeanie.

JEAN [*giggling*]: You not only a joker, Taj, but you too fresh-up with yourself! I mean, if you happen to be passing up by Rose Hill three o'clock this afternoon you never know what your luck might be... especially if you remember to bring that brooch along with you. I see it still in the glass case.

TAJ: Either the brooch or the sundial, I promise.

JEAN: But youself, Taj! Is how you expect me to wear that big thing on my hand and stand up in the sun waiting for a shadow?

At LALLA*'s house.*

LALLA: I get the news direct from the chairman, Johnny. That threat make them jump.

JOHNNY: I was just on the verge of my invention... All that gunpowder gone to waste, Lalla.

LALLA: Don't study that, man. Think, in a few weeks you could be bathing in the holy waters of the Ganges.

JOHNNY: You tell Gopaul yet?

LALLA: Look, him coming now.

JOHNNY [*quickly*]: Don't say nothing, eh, I want to test him out... [*As* GOPAUL *approaches*] Ah, Gopaul, we just call your name. You going to head the suicide march?

GOPAUL: Why me?

JOHNNY: We thought you might like the honour.

GOPAUL: Any news about the ship, Lalla?

LALLA: I was just telling Johnny…

JOHNNY: Why you so anxious about a ship?

GOPAUL: I been looking at this business from all angles, Lalla. A man like me, who prospering in Trinidad, shouldn't take no chances. I not as young as big-mouth Johnny here.

JOHNNY: Aha, you want to resign?

GOPAUL: I been talking to a lot of people, and plenty of them deciding they can't give up everything they have.

JOHNNY: What I tell you, Lalla? That suicide threat weed out the sheeps from the goats!

LALLA: Don't bother with Johnny, Gopaul… We getting a ship at last.

GOPAUL: True, Lalla?

LALLA: Yes. We only have a few more days.

GOPAUL: Well… It make no difference. I make up my mind to stay.

JOHNNY: You wasn't fooling me at all, Gopaul.

GOPAUL: I will still help out, though, if you want me to do anything… It have some old people, like Johnny, who can't make no headway in Trinidad and might be better off in India.

JOHNNY: Talk for yourself. Me and my jewel shop could buy you out any day. I stand firm, Lalla. How about you?

LALLA: Nothing going to stop me, personally.

JOHNNY: Spoken like a true Indian. It got some of we who give up our way of life for the passing attractions of Western society. But Indian civilisation was there thousands of years ago, and will still be there when other nations crumble in the dust…

Later that afternoon in JOHNNY's *shop. He is tinkering with some small instruments.* TAJ *is almost dozing in the heat.*

JOHNNY [*over sound of tinkering*]: What you doing there, boy? Sleeping?

TAJ [*starting from doze*]: Eh? You see me sleeping? [*Starts brisk hammering on metal*]

JOHNNY: I not looking but I could tell. Switch on the fan, it always make hot in the shop in the afternoon.

[TAJ *switches on the electric fan…* JULIA *comes into the shop, determined to have a serious talk with her father…*]

JULIA: Hello Pa.

JOHNNY [*astonished*]: Julia! What you doing here? Something happen home?

JULIA: No. I just come to see you.

JOHNNY: Well! This is the first time.

JULIA: Everything got to have a first time.

TAJ [*seizing the opportunity to get to Rose Hill*]: Am… I better take that gunpowder back, since you not using it.

JOHNNY: All right. I going to time you. If you come back late, you're fired!

TAJ [*mumbling as he goes*]: You should of been working for the Fire Brigade. [*He goes.*]

JOHNNY: Come behind the counter, girl. Don't stand there like a customer… Pull up Taj stool and sit down.

[JULIA *drags a stool close to* JOHNNY *and sits.*]

JULIA [*firmly*]: Pa, you and me got to have a talk.

JOHNNY: What about?

JULIA: Everything. I never get a chance to see you in the house. We live like strangers. I don't think you realise I am grown-up and have my own thoughts and feelings.

JOHNNY: I never hear you talk like this before.

JULIA: That's exactly what I'm saying… You and Ma always arguing, and I sitting down in the corner listening to the two of you.

JOHNNY: We'll settle all that when we go to India.

JULIA: Nobody ask me if I want to go.

JOHNNY: That's decided.

JULIA: Not for me. Trinidad is my country. I don't want to leave.

JOHNNY: Well, well! I didn't think the day would come when my own daughter talk to me like that… I better have a drink.

[*He uncorks a bottle and pours a drink.* JULIA *is looking on with disgust.*]

JOHNNY: Why you looking at me like that?

JULIA: You can't do without drink for once?

JOHNNY [*stoutly*]: Sure I can! You think I ain't got willpower? Watch… [*He pours the rum back in the bottle, and speaks as if to himself.*] Aye, is the first time I ever do a thing like this!

JULIA: Try and don't make it the last, Pa.

JOHNNY [*proud of himself*]: I not as drunkard and stupid as people think, you know… you want me to tell you a secret?

JULIA: What?

127

JOHNNY: One of these days I going to make an invention what will show everybody how smart I am.

JULIA: You won't invent nothing if you go on drinking.

JOHNNY [*thoughtful*]: You don't know... All these years... I been lonely, girl... Your mother ain't much company... always wanted a boy-child, but after you born she couldn't have no more children...

JULIA [*softly*]: You don't have to be lonely, Pa. Ain't you got me? Look how we talking now...

JOHNNY: I wish you was a boy!

JULIA: It's not my fault... I'm not useless, you know... and I love you, Pa. I know you have a soft heart under the big show you always making.

JOHNNY [*gruffly, masking emotion*]: Yes... Well, what you sweetening me up for now, eh? If is money you want...

JULIA: I don't want money. I just want you to treat me like a grown-up woman, and allow me to conduct my own life.

JOHNNY: What you want to do?

JULIA: Remain in Trinidad.

JOHNNY: We will discuss it when I come home.

JULIA: You going to be drunk then.

JOHNNY: No.

JULIA: You promise.

JOHNNY: Yes.

JULIA: Oh Pa, you don't know how happy that make me... You don't feel good, as we getting to understand one another?

JOHNNY: You lucky to catch me in a good mood!

JULIA: Then I better tell you about Govind...

JOHNNY: Who Govind that?

JULIA: The Indian boy who was home the other evening... that's who I love, Pa. I don't want anybody, not even you or Ma, to tell me what to do.

JOHNNY: How you know this Govind would make you a good husband? His father got money?

JULIA: Money ain't the only thing.

JOHNNY: Look, you catch me off-balance, coming here so sudden with all this...

JULIA: Why don't you see him, Pa? I could ask him to come this evening... At least that would be fair.

JOHNNY: All right, all right. You better go before I change my mind and have a drink...

JULIA: You want me to take the bottle before you get tempted?

JOHNNY: It got plenty where that come from... No, leave it. It will remind me.

JULIA [*hesitant, softly*]: Pa?

JOHNNY: You still here?

JULIA: Thanks for listening to me.

JOHNNY [*pretending wrath*]: Go from the shop before I chase you out! Coming here with all this rigmarole talk...

Later that evening at JOHNNY's *house.* GOVIND *and* JULIA *are waiting nervously for* JOHNNY *to come home.*

GOVIND: Suppose Johnny don't like me?

JULIA: Stop supposing and sit still, Govind! You making me nervous... I only hope he don't come home drunk.

GOVIND: It's only now I beginning to realise how little I have to offer you... What'll I tell him?

JULIA: I done my part! You've been after me for a long enough time to have it out with him.

GOVIND: All I got is this civil service job... You think we will manage?

JULIA: Stop worrying! Look, Pa coming now. He won't bite you, Govind.

GOVIND: Don't go! You better stay and give me some courage!

[JOHNNY *opens the door and comes in.* JULIA *greets him warmly with a kiss.*]

JULIA: Hello, Pa.

JOHNNY [*reacting to kiss*]: You want to smell my breath, or you really want to kiss me?

JULIA: You promised, and I believe you. This is Govind, Pa, you remember.

GOVIND [*nervous*]: Pleased to meet you, Mr. Johnny.

JOHNNY: You're the scamp who leading my daughter astray?

GOVIND [*nervous laugh*]: I... not exactly.

JOHNNY: Talk up, man. I don't like people who 'fraid to talk. You can't trust them.

GOVIND: What you want me to say, Mr. Johnny?

JOHNNY: What is your intentions? You want to get Julia in trouble and then make a beeline for the States or England?

GOVIND: I love Julia. And I have honourable intentions.

JOHNNY: Don't tell me nothing you read from some book, boy. Talk from your heart.

JULIA: Look, Pa...

JOHNNY: You keep quiet, girl. I want to hear what this boy got to say.

GOVIND: I know I not good enough for her, but I going to work hard...

JOHNNY: You right, you not good enough! My daughter not accustomed to no dhal and bhart you know. She come from rich respectable family... What work your father does?

GOVIND: He... drives a truck.

JOHNNY: Drive a truck!

JULIA: I not marrying Govind father, Pa...

JOHNNY: And what work you does yourself, pray?

GOVIND: I am a civil servant working for the Government.

JOHNNY: Rogues and vagabonds the whole lot of them... How much they pay you?

GOVIND: Not a lot, but we will manage... I expect to get a raise soon.

JOHNNY: Sooner than you think, when I kick you out of the house!

GOVIND [growing bold]: No need to take that attitude, Mr. Johnny.

JOHNNY: Ah! Now you want to tell me how to behave in my own house!

GOVIND: You'd rather Julia marry somebody she don't love and regret it all her life?

JOHNNY: She didn't hang she hat high, I could tell you.

GOVIND: That's between Julia and me, isn't it? We love one another and we want to marry. With or without your blessing.

JOHNNY [grudging admiration]: At least you got some guts, boy, to talk to me that way.

GOVIND: I have to tell you frankly, Mr. Johnny, Julia and me know each other a long time. It's not as if it's something sudden.

JULIA: I would never marry anybody but Govind, Pa.

JOHNNY: So... the both of you got it all plan already.

GOVIND: We hope you will give your permission, if not your blessing.

JOHNNY: H'mm. I tell you one thing in your favour... You got guts. I like somebody who could talk up for themselves.

130

JULIA: I knew you would be understanding, Pa.

JOHNNY: Hold your horses. I ain't saying yes, and I ain't saying no.

GOVIND: What are you saying, then?

JOHNNY: I will give the matter some thought... In the meantime, watch yourself and don't put Julia in any trouble, else I chop off your head with my own two hands.

GOVIND: I will look after her for the rest of my life.

JOHNNY: H'mm... We'll see... [*To* JULIA] Where your mother, girl?

JULIA: In the kitchen, Pa.

[JOHNNY *moves to the kitchen.*]

GOVIND [*low and anxious*]: What you think, Julia?

JULIA [*breathless*]: I think everything going to be all right... I hope.

In the kitchen.

MARY [*as he appears*]: You home early this evening.

JOHNNY: Yes. Sober too. What you know about this boy Govind family?

MARY: Nothing, except he have a big job with the Government.

JOHNNY: You better find out quick and let me know, because the ship coming to take we home... That rascal Gopaul back out at the last minute.

MARY: Gopaul not stupid like you. He got big business here, why he should leave it?

JOHNNY: I leaving mine.

MARY: I won't believe you going any place until we get on board that ship. Even now you likely to change your mind.

JOHNNY: Ha, that's what you think... I got a big crate and start packing up all my inventions and models... and I get a good offer for the jewel shop... Listen, you better have a talk with Julia. I don't know what get in she head. She was in the shop to see me.

MARY: Is about time you start being responsible.

JOHNNY: I got enough to worry about, and we only have a few days left... Say your last goodbyes, and keep that daughter of yours under control...

A few days later: a radio broadcast played in a country rumshop.

131

RADIO ANNOUNCER: …killed in an accident on the Eastern Main Road. That brings the road toll up to twenty deaths in only three months… The Back-to-India Committee has received an urgent telegram from the Prime Minister of India, exhorting them not to act hastily in leaving Trinidad. Far better, he suggested, that they remain and help to build up the island than return to an already over-populated India. The full text of the message reads as follows…

VOICE ONE: Oh Lord, I done sell my cow and patch of land!

VOICE TWO: I give notice that I leaving my job!

VOICE THREE: I wonder what the committee going to do now?

At Lalla's house.

JOHNNY: So what we going to do now, Lalla?

LALLA: This is something we didn't expect.

GOPAUL: It's a good thing I wasn't rushing like a madman like the rest of you.

JOHNNY: Don't lie, Gopaul. You back out because you thought I was going to blow you up with a bomb.

LALLA: We can't afford to treat the words of the Prime Minister lightly. But I actually seen the telegram itself, you know, and the way the news been spreading, is likely to misinterpretation.

JOHNNY: How you mean?

LALLA: Well, he didn't say that we *mustn't* come, he only advising against it, you follow?

JOHNNY: All the same, Lalla, to stalwart patriots like me, a word to the wise is sufficient, especially when it come from the mouth of our great leader himself.

LALLA: Anyway, we got to make sure that the people understand the message properly. That's the job the committee give us to do… You willing to help, Gopaul?

GOPAUL: I said so already.

LALLA: We ain't have much time. Today is Monday, and the ship sailing on Friday…. I want you to go down San Fernando and help. You, Johnny, tackle all the villages going right up to Toco. The job is to make certain the people know that they have a choice, that it is not an order from the Prime Minister. We distributing handbills all over the island explaining, but it got

132

some people who can't read. And don't prejudice anybody one way or another, let them make their own decision.

The day the ship is due to sail. JULIA *and* GOVIND *have come to visit* DR. WILKINS *at his office.*

WILKINS: Julia! And Govind! This is a nice surprise.

GOVIND: I hope we not disturbing you, Roy.

WILKINS: Of course not. I don't start work until Monday... Sorry about the seats, the office furniture hasn't turned up yet... I've been wondering how things are going with you... Have you come to say goodbye, Julia?

JULIA: No! Pa has come to his senses at last.

GOVIND: We still not sure, Julia.

WILKINS: But the ship sails this evening, doesn't it? I read the news.

JULIA: It sailing without me, anyway! Pa agree for me to stay. But up to now, we don't know what he himself is going to do.

GOVIND: I'll be glad if he get on that boat. A man like Johnny have so many moods, he might turn against us yet.

JULIA: I don't think so... Look how he stop drinking.

WILKINS: Is that right? It's as well. When I saw him that evening I could tell he wouldn't last long if he kept it up.

JULIA: I'm sure he'll go, it's only that he like to keep everybody in suspense. He got everything pack, but when Ma ask him he keep saying wait and see.

WILKINS: It shouldn't make a great difference for you and Govind now, anyway.

GOVIND: Nothing going to stop us from being together now, Roy. I been saving up my money and Julia is going to look for a job.

JULIA [*joking*]: Maybe I could be a receptionist for Roy!

WILKINS: Indeed, why not? I haven't got one yet.

JULIA: You're serious?

WILKINS: The job is yours if you want it, Julia. I'm sure you can do it. There isn't much to it, and you ought to know many of the local people. Give it a thought and let me know over the weekend... Perhaps you and Govind could have lunch with me on Sunday?

At the waterfront. Sounds of a large crowd can be heard. A RADIO REPORTER *is taping his commentary.*

RADIO REPORTER: ...Since last night these people have been coming to the capital from all parts of the island, and they have slept in sheds here on the waterfront. All their papers have been cleared, and it only remains for them to say their last farewells. What fate awaits them in distant India? It is a long voyage. Will any of them return? According to Mr. Lalla, who headed the sub-committee, everything was done to ensure the Prime Minister's warning was clearly understood by the Indian community... I can see Mr. Lalla now in the crowd, organising an orderly departure...

[*Enter* JOHNNY *and* LALLA.]

JOHNNY: ...you understand, Lalla? The way I see it, that telegram was like an order from the Prime Minister, and as a loyal and obedient subject...

LALLA: You don't have to explain, Johnny. I understand.

JOHNNY: Don't forget to write and let me know what the jewellery business is like over there. I mean, I would come by aeroplane! I could always make a little contraption to burn down the shop and collect insurance, if business is bad.

LALLA: Yes... well, is time to go on board. It's a pity you bring the wrong batteries for the record player.

JOHNNY: I don't know how I was so stupid. Somebody must of interfered with it at home.

LALLA: Never mind, we could still sing... Everybody line up an waiting, Johnny. We better say goodbye.

JOHNNY: I wish I was going with you, Lalla. Still, you might hear of me even in India when I finish my invention to harness Gravity.

LALLA: Keep at it, Johnny. One day you bound to succeed... Good-bye now. *Namaste.*

JOHNNY: *Namaste...* Goodbye, Lalla. [*Then loudly as* LALLA *moves off*] Long Live India!

[*The migrants start to sing the Indian National Anthem as they go on board. There is a brief silence. Then the ship's horn blasts three times, fading to the end.*]

THE END

THE HARVEST IN WILDERNESS

Characters

HARRILAL: Middle-aged Indian farmer.

SEETA: His wife. She dominates Harrilal; she is keen on material acquisitions and wants to leave cane life behind her. She tries to do this through her ambitions for her eldest son, Romesh.

ROMESH: Eldest son of Harrilal and Seeta. About twenty-one. Has just finished University in St. Augustine. He is Seeta's favourite. He is uncertain where his loyalties lie, between his family and the cane industry, and the life of Port of Spain.

TEEKA: Seeta's middle son and a more typical representative of the caneworkers. He is jealous of Romesh and for good cause.

POPO: The youngest son of Harrilal and Seeta. He is close to Balgobin, Harrilal's brother.

BALGOBIN: Harrilal's brother. Seeta refuses to acknowledge his existence due to some past secret. Balgobin and his cutlass 'Poya' represent the 'old' world of cane before mechanisation.

PETRA WHARTON: Romesh's 'white' girlfriend, a fellow student at the University. Seeta attempts to exploit her potential connections.

PUSHER: The 'idiot' of Wilderness who watches all; general scapegoat.

SOUZA: Shopkeeper in Wilderness.

MR. FORBES: Middle-aged Englishman in charge of the sugar company's laboratory. The company has bought up large tracts of Wilderness.

COMPANY MAN

FRIEND OF TEEKA

VILLAGERS

NEWSPAPERMEN

CAMERAMEN

Setting: Wilderness, a sugarcane village in Trinidad during the late 1960s, a period of transition. An East Indian community of sugar workers.

In the village of Wilderness, HARRILAL *has sold his land to the sugar company.* SEETA *has been using the money to modernise their house and set the family up with a car and other amenities for her son* ROMESH *who is just returning home after completing his University degree. One morning, she is getting ready to visit* ROMESH *in Port of Spain.* HARRILAL *is talking to her.*

HARRILAL: Seeta, you going to town this morning?

SEETA: You see me getting ready and you asking?

HARRILAL: Another new sari... h'mm... the way you been going through the money that we get from the Company for our land.

SEETA: If you look about you, Harrilal, you will see where all the money went. You living in a big house now, you have running water, electric light, new furniture, and a motor car.

HARRILAL: All of that is only because Romesh coming home. Sometimes I wonder if you remember we two other sons, Teeka and Popo... everything is Romesh, Romesh...

SEETA: You can't compare Romesh with them. He got education at the University, and going to work for the Company in the office. Not cutting cane and sweating in the fields like the rest of you!

HARRILAL [*grumbling*]: He should be coming to give a hand on the estate... You know the Company put me in charge of this section in Wilderness.

SEETA: You got Teeka to help you.

HARRILAL: I not so sure we could manage... [*Hesitant*] I, er... I was thinking that Balgobin could come to Wilderness and help out?

SEETA: Balgobin!

HARRILAL: He is one of the best canemen in Trinidad... It ain't have another man could swing a cutlass like my brother.

SEETA: That drunken old good-for-nothing! What make you call his name after all these years?

HARRILAL: I hear he working in La Gloria... that not so far from here... I don't know what you got against my brother. Ever since we married you refuse to let him come near the house.

SEETA [*vehemently*]: I don't want to see him again as long as I live!

HARRILAL: You and him used to be so thick before we married...

137

SEETA: Don't talk about the past! All that finish wit'... I just don't want him in Wilderness, that's all... and I waste enough time with you, I got to meet Romesh in town by midday... Teeka finish polishing the car?

HARRILAL: I will have a look as I go out... [*He goes off muttering to himself.*] ... All she ever think about is Romesh... I shouldn't of let her control the money in the first place.

[*A door opens and shuts. We hear the sounds of an outdoor atmosphere.*]

HARRILAL: Now finish Teeka? Your mother ready for the car.

TEEKA: Like all I will ever do is wash and polish the car. I ain't even get a chance to sit down inside it. I suppose she preserving it for the great Romesh.

HARRILAL: Never mind, your chance will come... Listen, I want you to go to La Gloria estate and look up your uncle Balgobin.

TEEKA: Lord! We ain't seen him for years! I thought he was dead?

HARRILAL: He must be past sixty-five and still going strong... must be all that rum he drink that holding his body together. Anyway, give him a message. Tell him I want to see him on some business... but not to come to the house.

TEEKA: Which part then?

HARRILAL: Tell him meet me in the shop here tomorrow morning.

TEEKA: Suppose he say no?

HARRILAL: He won't say no. Blood is blood, my own brother... and don't mention nothing to your mother. You know how she get on ignorant whenever Balgobin name mention...

The scene moves to the traffic and bustle of a shopping centre in Port of Spain where ROMESH *is waiting for* SEETA. *He dislikes his mother's possessiveness but is too weak to protest... She tries to appear worldly and speak proper English in his company...*

ROMESH: Ah, you've reached, Seeta.

SEETA [*coming up*]: Sorry if I'm late Romesh. You know what the blooming traffic is like... What about a kiss?

ROMESH: Not here... on this crowded pavement... Where's the car?

SEETA: I park over there, by the square.

ROMESH: Let's go... get out of the bustle... [*They start to move to the square.*] I hope you found some shade.

SEETA: Yes, just by that samaan tree... [*At the car now*] You drive, Romesh. [*They get in and shut the doors.*]

ROMESH [*starting and running the engine*]: Where are we going?

SEETA: What you want for lunch?

ROMESH: Oh anything.

SEETA: I don't like you to be like that. You should have an opinion and some ideas of your own.

ROMESH: Chinese, then. We could walk to that one in Queen Street, just over there.

SEETA: We'll go to that new one in St. Vincent Street, in the car. I have reasons to go there.

ROMESH [*driving off now*]: Why bother to ask me when you've already decided?

SEETA: You in a bad mood today... You not happy to see me?

ROMESH [*shortly*]: Of course.

SEETA: The reason why we going there is because it have a lot of good people does eat there.

ROMESH: Good people?

SEETA: You know... Senators and suchlike from the Government. People like that could help you out in your career... You got to make use of them... Think of the future, now that you finish University.

ROMESH: You know somebody?

SEETA: You don't have to know. Just be in the right place... Look under the dashboard there, I bought the latest Company bulletin for you. You read the others I sent?

ROMESH: All of them. Sugar and the Land, Sugar and the Economy, Sugar and the Common Market, and the Memorandum presented to the Tripartite Conference on Unemployment and Underdevelopment.

SEETA: Good... [*Pause*] We might be lucky to see some influential people in the restaurant.

ROMESH: We going to eat, or watch people?

SEETA: Is only politicians who making progress in this country, Romesh. Those who miss out still driving taxi and cutting cane... I want you to make a name for yourself. Though you going to work for the Company, is no reason you can't interest yourself in politics.

ROMESH: Let's talk about something else... How are things at home?

139

SEETA: The whole house done over! You can live in comfort now. You have your own room; I don't allow nobody to go in but myself.

ROMESH: Teeka still sleeps downstairs?

SEETA: Yes, he accustom to it... It's only you I bother about.

ROMESH [*as they arrive*]: Here we are... Better try and park in the shade.

Inside the bar...

SEETA: Let's have a drink. It's early yet, not so many people here...

ROMESH: All right. Let's sit in the lounge.

SEETA: That table near the door... We could see who coming in...

[*They sit and a waiter comes up.*]

WAITER: Yes please?

ROMESH: Two rum punches... plenty ice... and could we have the menu?

WAITER: Yes sir... [*He goes.*]

SEETA: When he come back, Romesh, ask for the manager.

ROMESH: What for?

SEETA: So he could attend to us himself.

ROMESH: Don't be so fussy.

SEETA: It's better to get personal attention... You have to learn to assert yourself, you know.

ROMESH [*as the waiter returns*]: Let's just have our drinks and look at the menu.

SEETA [*sipping drink*]: What you having?

ROMESH: My usual. Roast pork and fried rice.

SEETA: Again! You should try something new... The same thing every time.

ROMESH: I like roast pork and fried rice... We're not going to argue about the food?

SEETA: You're quick to quarrel today, I don't know what's wrong with you...

ROMESH: Well, you do keep on.

SEETA [*lightly*]: Never mind, I'll have the same as you. [*Pause as she sees a senator and a white girl come in.*] Lord, Romesh?

ROMESH: What?

SEETA [*voice low and excited*]: That is one of the senators! You don't

140

recognise him from his picture in the papers? He just come in with that white girl!

ROMESH: I recognise *her*.

SEETA: The *white* girl?

ROMESH: I wish you wouldn't say 'the white girl' like that... Yes, she used to be at the University.

SEETA: What's her name?

ROMESH: Petra. Petra Wharton.

SEETA: You know she to talk to?

ROMESH: We were very friendly... then we lost touch when she left.

SEETA: Call them over here for a drink.

ROMESH: Don't be silly.

SEETA: You can't understand she might introduce you to the Senator? You don't want to move in high company? That's always been the drawback of Indians, that's why we got no say in the island... We ain't even have a political party.

ROMESH: Ah, why can't you leave things alone, Seeta?

SEETA [*fiercely*]: Because you ain't going to be no country-bookie coolie boy! That's why you went to University! Ask them... for my sake, please?

ROMESH [*weakly*]: Well, too late now. They've gone straight in.

SEETA [*crossly*]: All your fault for dilly-dallying... and you notice how the manager himself looking after them?

ROMESH: You want another drink?

SEETA: No!

ROMESH: I'll have one at the bar myself... I'll send the waiter and you can order food... [*He goes.*]

WAITER [*coming to* SEETA]: Yes, madam... another drink?

SEETA: No... I want to order... Listen, you notice Senator Smith and that white girl who just come in?

WAITER: Oh yes?

SEETA: You could get us a table next to them? Or near up?

WAITER: Well, it might be hard...Lunchtime crowd coming in...

SEETA: I'll fix you up, don't worry.

WAITER: In that case, I might be able... You better give me the fix-up right now...

SEETA [*handing over the money*]: Here... that all right?

WAITER: Yes.

SEETA: Good. See what you could do for me... We'll have two full portions of number 12, number 8, number 7, number 4… and a nice big salad.

WAITER: That's a lot of food.

SEETA: I hope the Senator might join us, and if you give prompt service and look after us well, afterwards I'll fix you up again.

In the restaurant. ROMESH *and* SEETA *are sitting at their table…*

SEETA [*low*]: We right up close to them, Romesh! She must notice you now!

ROMESH: Oh, we've already seen each other.

SEETA: You did?

ROMESH: While you were busy taking in the other clientele… Here s our waiter now… [*As he puts out the food*] Wait! You must have the wrong table! What's all this?

SEETA: Hush! We could have them over here to eat with us… They only having drinks up to now.

ROMESH: You mean you ordered all this food hoping…

SEETA: Go over and ask them to join us, Romesh.

ROMESH: No!

SEETA: Please Romesh, please? For me?

ROMESH: But it's such an intrusion!

SEETA: Do it for me, please…

ROMESH [*weakening*]: Maybe they want to be alone.

SEETA: At least you could try…

ROMESH [*with a sigh*]: Ah… I suppose you'll keep on and on if I don't…

[*There is a slight pause as he goes and returns.*]

SEETA [*eagerly*]: What happen? They coming?

ROMESH [*shortly*]: No. They want to eat by themselves.

SEETA [*disappointed*]: This is a great opportunity… and we have all this food.

ROMESH [*savagely*]: Just stuff it down your guts. You've got money to waste, ordering all this… I'm only having what I told you…

SEETA: They might of come… [*They begin to eat. After a while…*] …She looking over here, Romesh… She been looking at you all the time.

ROMESH: Why you can't mind your own business? Or stick to minding mine, anyway?

142

SEETA: Everything I do is for you, Romesh, you know that…

ROMESH: Yes… Let's forget all about it.

SEETA: They're getting up… It look as if he going and leaving your friend!

ROMESH: It's got nothing to do with us…

SEETA: Yes! He gone, and she coming over here… Stand up, Romesh!

ROMESH: I'm not making a fool of myself. And this is the last time I'm coming here with you…

[PETRA *is at their table now. She is a pretty girl and attracted to* ROMESH…]

PETRA: Romesh! … No, don't get up! I just wanted to say how sorry I was we couldn't join you and your mother…

ROMESH: Seeta, this is Petra.

SEETA: Pleased to meet you… Won't you join us now?

PETRA: I've just eaten… I don't want to intrude…

ROMESH: It's no intrusion. Please… have some coffee with us.

PETRA: All right… [*Sits*] Just for a minute.

ROMESH: How've you been? The last time I saw you I was in a bit of a blur.

PETRA: You remember? It was that dance, the last night I spent at the University… You had so much to drink you couldn't see me home.

ROMESH: I tried to contact you after you left…

PETRA: I was in Tobago for a month or so.

ROMESH: What are you doing now?

PETRA: Helping my sister with a boutique in Frederick Street for the time being… And you?

SEETA: Romesh finish with University too… He going to be working for the sugar company… Miss Wharton, that…

PETRA: Petra, please.

SEETA: Then you call me Seeta… It make me feel young again! I was going to ask you if you know that Senator well… the one you was eating with?

PETRA: Who, Frank? He's a friend of the family… he's probably after an overdraft… My father works in banking.

SEETA: Oh. The bank, eh?

ROMESH: I was sorry about that last night, Petra.

143

SEETA [*slight pause*]: You young people must have a lot to talk, and I got some shopping to do. You don't have to come with me, Romesh. Stay and keep Petra company.

ROMESH [*with an edge of sarcasm*]: That's nice of you.

SEETA: I just want to have a word with you before I go…

PETRA [*jumping up*]: I was on my way to the ladies… I'll be back in a minute… [*She goes.*]

ROMESH [*bitterly*]: You want to take care of this too?

SEETA: You think I foolish? I only wanted to ask you if you have enough money… It would of embarrass you in front of Petra.

ROMESH [*hard laugh*]: Ha… what's a little more matter? I can manage with what I've got, thank you.

SEETA: Here. You better take this [*Passes him money*]. Twenty dollars. Just in case you might need it.

ROMESH: I don't want your money.

SEETA: Don't play stupid. Take it!

ROMESH: Well… all right.

SEETA: And what about the car? You might want to go some-where… I can always catch a taxi.

ROMESH: I think Petra's got her own. We can use that… though you're making something big of this meeting… I haven't seen her for a long time…

SEETA: Stay friends with she, Romesh! White people still have influence, don't mind all the talk about independence!

ROMESH: You'd better be going if you're going.

SEETA: All right… don't worry with the bill… I will attend to it as I go out… and remember what I say… [*She goes.*]

PETRA [*returning after a moment's pause*]: Has she gone, Romesh?

ROMESH: Yes, thank God! …How about a drink?

PETRA: After all that lunch!

ROMESH: I don't feel like it myself… The only way to get rid of that heavy feeling after a Chinese meal is to run round the block or do something active!

PETRA: Yes… or go for a swim…

ROMESH: Say, that's an idea! How about it?

PETRA: You forget I'm working.

ROMESH: Oh come on! You can phone your sister… Tell her you've met an old friend and you're taking the afternoon off!

PETRA: Where'll we go?

144

ROMESH: Maracas Bay? That's nearest. What do you say?

PETRA: I'm sorely tempted.

ROMESH: You got your car?

PETRA: Yes.

ROMESH: Come on then. We'll pick up something to wear on the way…

The scene moves to Maracas Bay. We hear the sound of distant surf, rustling coconut palms. PETRA *and* ROMESH *arrive…*

PETRA: Looks as if we've got the beach to ourselves.

ROMESH: Good… there's a place over there by those fishing boats where we can get some drinks to take with us… maybe some ice. We'll walk over…

[*Two* FISHERMEN *are drinking in the shop when they arrive…*]

BARMAN [*to* FISHERMEN]: Aye, you two fellars, don't go away with my glasses, eh… you fishermen thiefing them all the time… [*To* ROMESH] Yes mister?

ROMESH: You got any ice?

BARMAN: I run out. But the drinks cold.

ROMESH: Six cokes then, and a half of rum to take away.

[*The two* FISHERMEN *make remarks about* PETRA *as if in undertones, but loud enough for her to hear…*]

FISHERMAN ONE: Aye Joe! Look a white woman!

FISHERMAN TWO: A *white* woman?

FISHERMAN ONE: Yes, over there by the bar with that Indian fellar!

FISHERMAN TWO: But I thought we drive all the white people out of Trinidad since independence!

FISHERMAN ONE: Maybe she's a tourist Joe… Maybe she come Maracas Bay to catch fish?

ROMESH [*in a low aside to* PETRA]: Don't pay any attention, Petra. Just ignore them.

BARMAN [*putting drinks down*]: Here you are mister. That's two-seventy-five… [*Louder, to the* FISHERMEN] Why you-all like to interfere with people for? This gentleman and lady do you anything?

FISHERMAN ONE: But look at my contention here today! We just talking among ourselves here. We can't help it if people cock their ears to listen.

BARMAN [*to* ROMESH]: Thanks mister… You mustn't mind these ignorant fishermen. They don't know better.

ROMESH [*a bit brusquely*]: It's all right. Let's go, Petra.

PETRA [*fiercely, stopping at the* FISHERMEN'*s table as they go out*]: Listen you two! I was born and bred in Trinidad, and I have as much right as you to be living in this island! This is my home, and if it come to flinging back-yard remarks, I'm quite capable of taking care of myself! [*To* ROMESH] Come on, Romesh. [*They go out.*]

FISHERMAN ONE: You see Joe? You always get in trouble with your big mouth!

FISHERMAN TWO: You was the first to molest the woman. I was quietly sizing up that mini skirt when you began to talk.

Sounds of surf gently dying on the beach. ROMESH *and* PETRA *are lazing on the sands after their swim.*

PETRA [*lazily*]: What about a drink?

ROMESH: Who's going to get it?

PETRA: Forget it…

ROMESH: Feel like going back in?

PETRA: I'd rather just laze here on the beach… When you were small, did you use to throw sand on anyone who came out of the water, so they'd have to go in again?

ROMESH: You forget I'm a country boy… I never saw the sea until I grew up.

PETRA: What's it like in… I forget the place?

ROMESH: Wilderness?

PETRA: Yes. I never knew there was a place called that!

ROMESH: It's just a small sugarcane settlement, I don't blame you.

PETRA: That's where you're going to live now?

ROMESH: Yes. It's not far from the Company offices where I'd be working… After a few months they may send me to England for further training… if Seeta agrees.

PETRA: Your mother?

ROMESH: Yes. She would like to run my life for me.

PETRA: She seemed nice…

ROMESH: You don't know her… She doesn't give me a chance to breathe. I have to dance to her tune, and yet she tries to give the impression I'm free to do what I like… You know what's her latest idea? To set me up in politics!

146

PETRA: Some parents like that...

ROMESH: Ah, but there's only one Seeta! She's clever, always manages to get her own way in the end. You should see how she dominates the family. My father hardly says a word... he's like a stranger to me. And my brother Teeka... sometimes I'm sorry for him. It seems I've had all the opportunities at his expense.

PETRA: You sound like her favourite?

ROMESH: Is that what you call being trapped in a net as if you can't escape? Even here, now, on this beach, it's as if I could feel her presence... You know it wouldn't surprise me to see her walking down through the coconut trees...

PETRA: Let's talk about something else, then... your job?

ROMESH: I'll be in the lab, I expect, experimenting with sugar.

PETRA: What sort of experiment?

ROMESH: You really want to know? There's a premium in the market on a certain grade of yellow sugar the Company has been trying to manufacture... I've been working on one or two ideas while I was at the University... Oh damn!

PETRA: What, a mosquito?

ROMESH: Mosquito, hell! Here we are, two full-blooded young people on a lonely beach talking about sugar! Come closer... that's better.

PETRA [*in a softer mood now*]: What shall we talk about then?

ROMESH: We shan't talk at all... [*He kisses her.*]

PETRA [*soft laugh*]: We must, before there's trouble.

ROMESH: Are you tied up with anybody?

PETRA: No-o.

ROMESH: Good.

PETRA: But you are.

ROMESH: Me?

PETRA: Yes. With your mother.

ROMESH: There we go again! Can't we leave her out of anything?

PETRA: You started it.

ROMESH: And I'm finishing it... no more talk...

PETRA [*soft cry*]: Wait... oh...

[*Fade up surf and fade out...*]

147

We move to a village street in Wilderness next morning. HARRILAL *arrives to meet* BALGOBIN. *He stops at the shop entrance for a word with* PUSHER, *the village 'idiot'.*

HARRILAL: Aye, Pusher.

PUSHER: Morning, Mr. Harrilal.

HARRILAL: You been sitting in front the shop all morning: anybody ask for me?

PUSHER: No. Unless they come when I was making my rounds of the village… You know I got to check up every morning and see that things okay…

HARRILAL [*sarcastic*]: I hope you find things to your satisfaction, Mr. Pusher?

PUSHER: Some of the drains have so much weeds growing in them the water collecting and making mosquitoes. I think we have to do something about that.

HARRILAL: Anything else?

PUSHER: I notice some of the men was late for work… In my days every man had to turn out on time and work hard.

HARRILAL: Yes, like you, sitting down here in front the shop all day long and minding people business. You know what you should do, Pusher?

PUSHER: What?

HARRILAL: Look for a shady spot and drop dead!… Shift that soapbox, you blocking the entrance…

[HARRILAL *goes into the shop and raps on the counter.*]

HARRILAL [*to the shopkeeper*]: Souza, anybody been asking for me?

SOUZA: No.

HARRILAL: Well… maybe he ain't come yet.

SOUZA: Who?

HARRILAL: My brother, coming to work in Wilderness.

SOUZA: I never knew you had a brother.

HARRILAL: If you count up all the things you don't know, you will never finish… Give me a nip in the meantime whilst I waiting for him.

PUSHER [*from the doorway as* SOUZA *gets the drink*]: I see a stranger in Wilderness!

HARRILAL: What he look like?

148

PUSHER: Tall... thin... like one hand longer than the other... No, is a cutlass he carrying...

HARRILAL: Sounds like him. Balgobin don't part company with his cutlass... [*To* SOUZA] ... Bring another glass, Souza, and open up a bottle instead...

[BALGOBIN *enters the shop. He is very old and cynical, but still wiry and tough. He has a chronic cough and throughout the play coughs from time to time.*]

BALGOBIN: Aye, Harrilal!

HARRILAL: Glad to see you, Balgobin!

BALGOBIN: Why?

HARRILAL: Why? I mean after such a longtime... must be years...

BALGOBIN: We should be glad when we part, not when we meet.

HARRILAL: Yes, I suppose so... Have a drink, man. You must be thirsty from the hot sun. [*Pours for him*] How things going for you in La Gloria? You married? You got family?

BALGOBIN [*taking a long swig*]: Ah... how you know I was in La Gloria?

HARRILAL: Easy for a man like me to find out where the greatest caneman in Trinidad working.

BALGOBIN: They know about me even in a little kiss-me-arse estate like Wilderness, eh?

HARRILAL: We not as small as you think... We part of the Company now, since I sell my land.

BALGOBIN: Trust people like you to sell out to the Company.

HARRILAL: I get a good price. And a big position, too. In charge of this section around here. In fact that's why I wanted to see you... Let's move over to that table in the corner over there, in case customers come in.

[*They move and settle in the corner.* BALGOBIN *coughs.*]

HARRILAL: This is better. Keep your voice down when you talk... You sound like you have a bad cough?

BALGOBIN: We not here to discuss my ailments.

HARRILAL: Well, as I was saying, I got this big supervising job, and to put it short, I want you to help me out, as I can't manage on my own. My head too hot since we come into money.

BALGOBIN: How you mean?

HARRILAL: Seeta gone mad. She build a new house, she buy car, she gallivanting all about playing lady.

BALGOBIN: That's what she always wanted from what I could remember... [*Musing tone*] Seeta always had big ambition, that's why she and me never get on... that's why she choose you to married, Harrilal, more than twenty years ago that was.

HARRILAL: Yes, and when we married, you went off like a bullet and you never come to visit the family. I got three sons, you know.

BALGOBIN: Three? I only hear about Teeka, and that other one, am, Romesh his name is?

HARRILAL: First was Romesh, who went to University and was working in the Company office, then Teeka, who helps me with the work, and then the little boy Popo, who still going to school.

BALGOBIN: So much for your family history. Let's get down to business.

HARRILAL [*replenishing drinks*]: The position is this, Balgobin. I want you to stay and work in Wilderness. Better pay than you get in La Gloria.

BALGOBIN: It sounds tempting. And now that you got a big house and thing, at least I could have a decent roof over my head... dead in comfort in my old age...

HARRILAL: Ah, that's the one thing... the way how Seeta get on, as if she don't want to set eye on you again. I mean, for myself, you welcome to stay by me... You could of sleep downstairs with Teeka, but Seeta...

BALGOBIN [*interrupting*]: On second thoughts I wouldn't live by you if you pay me!

HARRILAL [*relieved*]: I know you rather be by yourself... I got a small hut not far from here.

BALGOBIN: I live rough all my life... me and Poya...

HARRILAL: Poya?

BALGOBIN: Yes, my cutlass here.

HARRILAL: Oh yes, I forget you keep it with you all the time.

BALGOBIN: I does sleep with it. [*Addressing the cutlass*] We never parted, eh, Poya? Have a little drink... [*He drips some rum on the blade.*]

HARRILAL: You wasting good rum pouring it on the cutlass, man!

BALGOBIN [*to cutlass*]: You hear what Harrilal saying, Poya? He don't know what good friends we is... how much cane we cut together all over Trinidad... [*To* HARRILAL] Pass your thumb over this blade, Harrilal... you ever feel a edge like that?

150

HARRILAL [*testing*]: Jeez! I cut my hand!

BALGOBIN [*chuckles*]: Maybe Poya don't like you... Maybe he don't want to stay in Wilderness to help out my stupid brother who can't manage his own affairs, either in the canefield or his own house... [*He has a fit of coughing.*]

HARRILAL: Like you can't control that cough, man! You sure you in good health?

BALGOBIN: Let's have a man-to-man fight and see. Cutlass to cutlass.

HARRILAL: Put it aside, man, don't wave it so near me. And let me know what you decide.

BALGOBIN: I got conditions if I stay here.

HARRILAL: Like what?

BALGOBIN: I am my own boss. I not taking orders from anybody, including you.

HARRILAL: I don't mind... just to have you around will ease me up with the problems I have... but one more thing.

BALGOBIN: What?

HARRILAL: Try and keep out of Seeta way... She going to kick up more hell when she find out I bring you to the estate.

BALGOBIN: You could tell Seeta to keep out of my way. I don't want to see she either.

HARRILAL: Good, then. I got some things to attend to now... I will see you in the fields later?

BALGOBIN: That depends on my mood... and before you go, you better get another half bottle of rum for me... I might as well get what I could out of this blood money the Company give you...

A few days later, ROMESH *goes in to see* MR. FORBES, *a middle-aged Englishman who is in charge of the laboratory. He knocks at the door.*

FORBES: Come in... Ah, Romesh, nice to see you... Shut the door... Sit down... Smoke if you like.

ROMESH [*sitting and lighting a cigarette*]: I came to see you about that project I put forward, Mr. Forbes. It's been two weeks now, and I haven't heard anything.

FORBES: Patience, my boy. Things take time round here. You haven't been with us long enough to find out, but you'll learn... I've got several ideas that are years old and I've heard nothing more about them... thank goodness.

ROMESH: I'd like to get on with something... I feel as if I'm wasting time in the lab, just sitting around most of the time.

FORBES: What was that proposal again?

ROMESH: About yellow sugar...

FORBES: Oh yes. I read your report on what you were doing at University... We've been doing work on that idea for a long time. We're not prepared to spend time or money on preliminary research which has been done already.

ROMESH: Oh. Well...

FORBES: Sit down. I haven't finished. I have an interest personally... I did a lot of spade work myself, and I'm intrigued with your idea about a negative cause.

ROMESH [*eagerly*]: That's what I mean. I read all the reports on what you did... but they were all positive.

FORBES: Explain what you mean.

ROMESH: Well, we know it isn't the soil. Nor the climate or any species of cane we haven't been able to grow. And you've tried fertilisers...

FORBES: Yes, yes... Get to the point.

ROMESH: I believe it is in the actual processing in the factory from cane to sugar that the crystals undergo the change or changes that make them get their particular colour and texture and flavour.

FORBES: All that's nothing new. We've experimented exhaustively with all the processing stages. With the most modern equipment.

ROMESH: Yes, but you've been looking for some positive formula incorporating some secret ingredient. I don't think it's that at all.

FORBES: What do you think it is?

ROMESH: I want to look for something negative. Suppose, somewhere along the line in their processing, the people who make this type of sugar are accidentally introducing some bacteria?

FORBES: Accidentally?

ROMESH: Originally, anyway. Of course, since then they've been reproducing under identical conditions, with the same equipment all the time. We could limit our research to the kinds of bacteria we usually get rid of.

FORBES: H'mm... an interesting theory.

ROMESH: And we won't be covering ground already investigated..

FORBES [*thoughtful pause*]: I see from your record that you don't play cricket!

ROMESH [*puzzled*]: Cricket?

FORBES: Yes.

ROMESH: Well, no... but what...

FORBES: It's a great game, you know. You're the first Trinidadian I met who doesn't play. We have a fine side here in the Company. I don't suppose you happen to know the latest score, anyway?

ROMESH: Score?

FORBES: The Test score, man. There's a West Indies team playing in England now. I forgot to bring my transistor to work this morning.

ROMESH: I'm sorry, but...

FORBES: Never mind. I only mentioned it because we work as a team in the lab... This idea of yours, you want to go ahead on your own?

ROMESH: Oh, I see what you're getting at... No, of course not... whatever you like.

FORBES: I think I'll leave you to it, anyway. I won't mention anything until you come up with something posit... I mean negative. How long do you think?

ROMESH: I can start some experiments right away.

FORBES: Good. Let me have a report when you think you've found something new.

ROMESH: Thank you, Mr. Forbes... [*He goes.*]

FORBES [*muttering to himself*]: H'mm... long arms, tall build... what a bowler he'd make... Can't understand why he hasn't an interest in the game...

Fade on FORBES... *to* SEETA, *who wants to use* PETRA *to further* ROMESH's *interests... One morning she phones her...*

PETRA: Hello...Calypso Boutique.

SEETA: Hello... is that Petra?

PETRA: Yes... Who is it?

SEETA: It's me, Seeta, remember? Romesh's mother...

PETRA: Oh yes?

SEETA: I wanted to come and see you.

PETRA: Is anything wrong? Romesh...

SEETA: No... just to have a friendly little chat, if you don't mind?

153

PETRA: Of course not… but what's it about?

SEETA: I'll tell you when I see you… I driving to town tomorrow. Romesh usually use the car to go to work, but he promise to let me have it… I getting a small one for myself soon… he tell you?

PETRA: No…

SEETA: We really need two cars, between him and me! Anyway, tomorrow all right?

PETRA: What time?

SEETA: About eleven o'clock? We could meet in the Queen's Park Hotel around the Savannah… You won't have no trouble taking time off?

PETRA: No. That'll be all right.

SEETA: Oh! I nearly forget! I could ask you a personal question?

PETRA [*slight hesitation*]: What is it?

SEETA: Don't laugh, but I want to know your bust measurement.

PETRA: My bust!

SEETA: Please, I have a reason.

PETRA: Well, it's thirty-six.

SEETA: Good. See you tomorrow then. Goodbye. [*She puts the receiver down.*]

The hotel next morning…

SEETA: Ah Petra, good morning!

PETRA [*coming up*]: Hello Seeta.

SEETA: I got a table in that corner… You like lime punch? That's what I'm having.

PETRA: Just the thing. It's so hot this morning…

SEETA: You go and sit down while I tell the waiter… [*The waiter brings the drinks.*] …This is nice and cold… [*Producing a paper parcel*] …Here, this is for you.

PETRA: Oh? Something from Romesh?

SEETA: No. He don't even know about it. Just a little present from me. A little surprise for you… Open it?

PETRA [*opening the parcel*]: Don't tell me… Oh, a sari?

SEETA: You like it? I notice when we meet how you admire my sari!

PETRA: What gorgeous colours! And this piece… what's it?

SEETA: That's the choli, to go with the sari.

PETRA: Oh-h, so that's why you wanted my bust measurements!

SEETA: Yes… you have a nice figure, Petra, it should fit you…

154

PETRA: I don't know what to say... it's lovely! Really Seeta, you shouldn't have bothered.

SEETA: I get it from India, you know... the sari, I mean. I orders all my clothes from there, you know.

PETRA: I wish I could try it on right now! I'll wear it this evening, anyway... I'm seeing Romesh.

SEETA: Yes, I know. He's been spending more time with you than in Wilderness! Still, I don't blame him with a pretty girl like you.

PETRA: If you're handing out compliments, when I first saw you with Romesh, I thought you were his girl friend! Honestly.

SEETA [*flattered*]: In truth?

PETRA: Either that, or his sister... [*Dismayed now*] Oh dear!

SEETA: What happen?

PETRA: I promised him that if ever you and I were alone, we'd never mention his name!

SEETA: That's one fault Romesh have... he too modest, and shy. What else we would talk about but him? That's why I come to see you, Petra... I know the young generation these days prefer to live their own way, but Romesh is a most important part of my life, and I got to look after him... Tell me something... You like him?

PETRA: Of course.

SEETA: You *love* him? [*As* PETRA *hesitates*] ...You might think I shouldn't interfere, but I have a purpose... You have a lot of boy friends, I suppose?

PETRA: A few.

SEETA: But Romesh is the one you serious about? I know he serious about you, because the moment I call your name he stop talking.

PETRA [*uneasy laugh*]: Really Seeta... Romesh is a big boy now, and capable of looking after himself... Why do you bother?

SEETA: I want to help him. And if you don't love him, you might as well say straight out, and save me a lot of talk.

PETRA: Let me hear what you have to say first, before I commit myself.

SEETA: I want him to get along and make a name for himself.

PETRA: I'd like to see him happy too.

SEETA: Then listen: we going to have a by-election in our district for the local Council, and I want to put Romesh up for the seat.

PETRA: He isn't interested in politics, is he?

SEETA: The trouble with Romesh is he got to be pushed... Don't forget he got University education.

PETRA: I don't know how much that counts for these days.

SEETA: Everything count, and everything helps. I want to see his head in the right direction. And you could help if you want.

PETRA: How? What can I do?

SEETA: You remember that Senator you was having lunch with the day I meet you in that Chinese restaurant?

PETRA: He's a friend of my father...

SEETA: Still, you know him. Listen, if you just mention Romesh name and get him to put in a word here and there... little things like that put a lot of stupid people in power in Trinidad, girl... I know what I talking about. And another thing is the University.

PETRA: How does that come in?

SEETA: These days students have a lot of influence, and they putting a finger in every pie. Both you and Romesh was there, and I hope you still have friends among them who could do something...

PETRA: But what?

SEETA: I not rightly sure... strike, protest, demand Romesh get the seat... walk about town with placards... it got a lot they could do.

PETRA: Look, Seeta, does Romesh know what you're planning?

SEETA: He always agree with what I do.

PETRA: But oughtn't you to discuss it with him?

SEETA: It got nothing to discuss. I know what best for him.

PETRA [with a pause]: I can't make any promises, Seeta. I don't know the first thing about politics, to begin with... I'll have to talk to Romesh first. Perhaps I do love him, and we both... you and I, I mean... want the same thing. But I want to go about it my own way.

SEETA: All right. Tell him if you like, it won't make no difference.

PETRA: I will. When I see him this evening. Now let's talk about something else for a change, please.

SEETA: When you coming to Wilderness to see the place?

PETRA: Romesh hasn't asked me.

SEETA: Well, I asking... You must come soon. We fix up the whole house, and Romesh got the best room.

PETRA: What about your other children?

SEETA: You mean Teeka and Popo? Neither of them got Romesh's brain... They only fit for the canefields.

PETRA: And Romesh's father?

SEETA [*hesitant*]: His father?

PETRA: Yes, Harrilal.

SEETA: I... I got to do all Harrilal thinking for him... [*Firmer now*]...
You will meet all of them when you come. Excepting that
vagabond Balgobin.

PETRA: That's the wild uncle? Romesh told me the story.

SEETA [*quickly*]: What story?

PETRA: How you have him banned from the house... and had a big
quarrel with Harrilal about bringing him to Wilderness.

SEETA: Oh that. Nothing else?

PETRA: Only that he didn't know this uncle at all, and had never
spoken to him. You don't even want his name mentioned in the
house!

SEETA: A good thing too... Every family got a black sheep, and
Balgobin is our one. He will only drag down Romesh and bring
disgrace on him. I don't want the two of them to have anything
at all to do with one another.

PETRA: You sound very bitter about him?

SEETA: He too worthless! He deserve to be living in a mud hut in the
bush, while I have a big house and car. It must *grind* him to see
the difference. But I did always know that he would never
make anything of his life... [*In a softer tone now*] Anyway, you
mustn't think that I got no heart at all... He doesn't starve. I
send Popo over with some food every evening, just out of
human kindness.

PETRA: Aren't you afraid he might be a bad influence on the little
boy?

SEETA: Who care about Popo? As long as he don't interfere with me
or Romesh, he could do anything he like... But let's forget him,
he ain't worth talking about... You know how to put on a sari?
You must try and get the pleats even before you tuck the end in
the waist...

PETRA: It's the... choli? I'm worried about.

SEETA: Just wear it like a blouse... some women doesn't wear any
bra with it, as it suppose to fit tight and snug....

*Later that night in Wilderness. Insects are chirruping and frogs croaking
as* POPO *arrives with some food at* BALGOBIN's *hut.*

POPO [*calling*]: Uncle! [*Distant coughing from the hut*] Uncle Balgobin!

BALGOBIN [*coming*]: All right boy, I hear you. You think I dead?

POPO: I bring food.

BALGOBIN: Put it there on the step. I will eat it later.

POPO: Mai say to see you eat it while it hot… nice talcurry with saltfish in it…

BALGOBIN: Your mother can't tell me when to eat, boy. Just put it there. [*Coughs*]

POPO: The cough not getting better?

BALGOBIN: Don't worry. When you get an old man and dead, I will still be alive.

POPO: Yes, Uncle. It would take more than a little cough to kill you.

BALGOBIN [*a little brighter*]: Well, what you waiting for, Popo? I suppose you want to see Poya, eh?

POPO [*eagerly*]: Yes!

BALGOBIN: Look him in the corner inside. Bring him out. It still got some light in the sky… [POPO *returns with the cutlass.*] Boy! How much time I got to tell you, don't hold a cutlass with the edge turn to you? Suppose you trip and fall?

POPO: Sorry, Uncle.

BALGOBIN: All right. Now show me what you do when you see a patch of cane.

POPO [*wielding cutlass*]: I do so… so… and so…

BALGOBIN: You lie. That ain't what I teach you. Give it to me… [*Takes cutlass, demonstrates*] When you do so, and so, and then so, you cut three canes at one time… and right away, even as you cut the cane down, you start planting for next year… Here, you show me. The bullock cart waiting, and the woman coming up fast behind you to bundle and load up. You got to work fast, because the more loads the driver take to the factory, the more pay they get…

POPO [*active with the cutlass*]: So… and so… and so…

BALGOBIN: Good. Good. But don't cut too near the top. Remember you want the cane tops for fodder for the animals.

POPO: You think I will make a good caneman, Uncle?

BALGOBIN: You will be as good as me. You can't get better than that. Take a little rest now.

POPO: All right… Tell me about the time when you-one tackled a field of cane and finish before the other workers could even get

158

started... You remember, it was on the estate in Cross Crossing...

BALGOBIN: Ah-h, them was days when a man was a man... Nobody don't work like that again. They get sweeten up and lazy.

POPO: That's true, Uncle... You know what I hear?

BALGOBIN: What?

POPO: I hear it got harvesting machines what could do the work of eighty-ninety men!

BALGOBIN: That is only nancy-story, boy. No machine could work like a man.

POPO: And I hear the Company going to try out one right here in Wilderness!

BALGOBIN: Which part you pick up all that nonsense?

POPO: Oh, I got my ears open wide! I does listen to everything they say in the house... That's how I know you is a vagabond, and Mai won't let you come near the house...

BALGOBIN: She does talk so about me?

POPO: Only when she in a bad mood and quarrelling... but one day Romesh was asking and she tell him to have nothing to do with you... You know another thing?

BALGOBIN: What?

POPO [*in an awed whisper*]: Romesh got a white girl friend in Port of Spain!

BALGOBIN: White, you say?

POPO: Yes. Nearly every evening he does take the car and drive to town... He got this big job with the Company, you know... I think he in charge of a lab, experimenting with sugar.

BALGOBIN: Experimenting! He should be sweating in the field like his brother Teeka. That's the only way to learn about cane.

POPO: Mai don't want him to do no labouring work! She say the Company going to send him to England soon! It have cane in England, Uncle?

BALGOBIN: I suppose so. Why else would they send him there?

POPO: My teacher in school say cane don't grow in England, because the sun doesn't shine there at all... I will miss Romesh when he go. Between him and Teeka, I prefer him. Mai favour him too. She say she got BIG plans for him.

BALGOBIN [*grunts*]: Huh. I don't know why you listen to all this stupidness and come to tell me. I not interested.

159

POPO: Not even about the harvest machine?

BALGOBIN: That's only idle talk, boy.

POPO: Well I hear Romesh telling Mai.

BALGOBIN: And I tell you that no machine could cut cane like Poya here.

POPO: I hear Romesh say that a time will come when it won't need no men in the fields, that machine would do all the work… He say I must learn all my lessons good, so I won't have to go out in the hot sun to cut cane.

BALGOBIN [*abruptly*]: You better go home, boy. Your mother must be waiting on you.

POPO: All right… You want me to get some medicine from the doctor-shop for your cough?

BALGOBIN: No. Cane juice and rum is the best thing.

POPO: And when I come tomorrow, you will let me practice with Poya again?

BALGOBIN: Yes. But go now and leave me in peace… [*Coughs*]

The scene changes to a street in Port of Spain where ROMESH *has just met* PETRA, *and is pleasantly surprised to see her in the sari…*

ROMESH: Hi! Where'd you get the sari?

PETRA: You like it?

ROMESH: You look lovely… Is it from your sister's boutique?

PETRA: It's a present.

ROMESH [*facetious*]: Taking gifts from strange men, eh?

PETRA [*little laugh*]: You'll never guess who gave me… Seeta.

ROMESH: Seeta!

PETRA: She came to see me this morning.

ROMESH [*sharply*]: What for?

PETRA: Let's drive up Chancellor Hill where it's quiet.

ROMESH: I thought we were going to eat at that new restaurant?

PETRA: We could eat afterwards.

ROMESH: But what did she want?

PETRA: Keep your temper, you haven't even heard what I have to say.

ROMESH: But what business could she have with you? What right has she got to see you?

PETRA: Romesh, will you calm down and listen?

ROMESH [*with effort*]: All right... [*Lights two cigarettes*] ...Here you are... I'm calm now.

PETRA [*smoking*]: Thanks. Relax and listen to me.

ROMESH: Okay, okay, just make a start.

PETRA: In my own time. I'm thinking.

ROMESH: If it's giving you pleasure, go right ahead.

PETRA: What I mean is, I understand you more now. I remember at University you were so much by yourself... alone, as if you hadn't a single friend.

ROMESH: What's all this got to do with Seeta's visit?

PETRA: You and your mother are inseparable, Romesh. I can't think of one without the other.

ROMESH [*making a rude sound*]: Chut... is that what she came to tell you?

PETRA: Not exactly. But you say it even better than she does.

ROMESH: Say what better?

PETRA: Look at you now! From the moment I told you Seeta's given me this sari, you've been boiling inside with some strong emotion I can't define. Tell me something. Couldn't you have felt it was nice and gracious of her to come to see me, and to make me happy with a small gift?

ROMESH: You don't know Seeta, Petra. It just wouldn't be anything I would wish for. Let me tell you again. That woman has been riding me from the time I was a child. God knows how I've tried to shake her off my back. We've had countless quarrels since I went home. I haven't told you yet, but I'm going to leave Wilderness. I can't bear to live in the same house.

PETRA [*quickly*]: When?

ROMESH [*edge of hesitancy*]: I... I... I'm deciding.

PETRA: Have you told Seeta?

ROMESH: Not yet.

PETRA: Are you going to tell her?

ROMESH [*weak laugh*]: Oh come on, give me a chance! I don't want to hurt her.

PETRA: Seeta has moved with the times, Romesh. She doesn't expect or want the old-fashioned Indian family customs.

ROMESH [*slight sarcasm*]: It was sociology you graduated in?

PETRA: Don't make fun. I'm serious. She knows about students' revolts and black power and trips to the moon. You could walk out tomorrow if you wanted to, and she would reconcile herself. Look how she treats your Uncle Balgobin, for instance.

ROMESH: You two must have had quite a talk. Did she tell you my bed lies east-west too?

PETRA: You know quite well what I'm getting at.

ROMESH: We're heading for a quarrel, that's what I know.

PETRA [*with spirit*]: Then let's quarrel if it'll help to get to the truth!

ROMESH: What truth?

PETRA: Seeta and you, that's what! You love her, and she loves you. And I don't mean any mother-son love either. It's some sort of fixation thing going on between you... Can't you see that?

ROMESH [*talking out a laugh, with a pause*]: Ha-hah-ha.

PETRA: Don't try to avoid the issue.

ROMESH: What issue you're talking about?

PETRA: Face it, Romesh. Seeta is going to live your life for you and you're going to let her. Be honest. She's done it all the time, and you've accepted the situation.

ROMESH: Okay, so she's pushed me around, I grant you... But what's this fixation talk? You're not suggesting anything?

PETRA: Should I?

ROMESH: Don't throw it back!

PETRA: These things happen... You could have thoughts which have nothing to do with the fact that she's your mother... I never met an Indian before who referred to his mother all the time by her first name!

ROMESH [*hard laugh*]: What? I hate her! I h-a-t-e her!

PETRA: You've been trying so hard to convince me of that I'm beginning to wonder...

[*He makes a gesture to touch her.*]

No, don't touch me now! That's what Seeta does, isn't it? Strokes your hand or pats your head when you're angry. You told me so yourself!

ROMESH [*a little calmer*]: All right. Let's get back to why she wanted to see you.

PETRA: She has ambitions for you. She wants you to go into politics. There's going to be a by-election in your district.

ROMESH: And where do you fit in all this?

PETRA: You know, don't you, but you're scared of saying it... a white girl in Port of Spain, from the University, whose father happens to know a few influential people... she asked me to spread your name.

ROMESH: And all she gave you was a sari?

PETRA: I won't let you make me angry... I want to know how you feel about Seeta, and you'd better tell me the truth right now, before it's too late.

ROMESH [*worked up*]: I'll tell you... I hate her so much that I feel like strangling her... I do all I could to keep out of her way... Every morning, in Wilderness, when she prepares my breakfast and I force it down, I want to spew it on my way to work.

PETRA: But you don't do you?

ROMESH [*going on*]: ...and I'm going to leave, Petra. I swear it. My God, she couldn't even let me have a little happiness with you... I wish you'd phoned me at work to tell me she was coming, so that I could have been there to ram her conceit and selfishness down her throat!

PETRA [*quietly*]: Romesh... you must decide if you're going to leave Wilderness. It matters, for us...

ROMESH: I told you... I'm getting out... if she thinks I'm going to be like the rest of them... Harrilal, my own father who can't breathe a word in her presence... Teeka, whom she treats like a common field labourer... my Uncle Balgobin...

PETRA: She's forbidden you to see him, hasn't she?

ROMESH: Forbidden?

PETRA: It's all the same... Listen, Romesh, we're finished you know, unless you make up your mind. I don't want to be involved in your family affairs.

ROMESH: I'm leaving Wilderness.

PETRA: Don't say it. Do it! I can't trust your feelings while you're under her spell... It sounds melodramatic but that's what it is.

ROMESH: I needed something like this to help me to make up my mind, Petra. I'm going to have a showdown with her as soon as I get back, and clear out.

PETRA: It shouldn't be hard to get a room in town.

ROMESH: No. I'll telephone you as soon as I have it out with her.

PETRA: You're sure? You'll do it tonight?

ROMESH: You can expect a call from me exactly [*Glances at watch*] ...let's see... we still have to eat... it's eight thirty now... Give me three quarters of an hour to drive back home. It'll be near midnight.

PETRA: It's an important call, I'll wait up. You won't disappoint me?

ROMESH: No... I've half a mind to forget about eating and go back right now.

PETRA: I'm starving.

ROMESH: We'd better eat then... and I could do with some heavy double rums to gather my thoughts...

PETRA: Make sure they're not scattered instead...

That same evening TEEKA *is entertaining a* FRIEND *on the verandah of the house in Wilderness. They are drinking...*

FRIEND: Aye, boy Teeka, we been sitting down here in your gallery drinking a long time. I better go before somebody come back...

TEEKA: Don't worry man. Everybody gone out... This is the only chance I does get to come up here and relax, and drink some of the special liquors they have hide up in the house. Have another...

FRIEND [*as* TEEKA *fills glasses*]: Romesh in town again?

TEEKA: As usual... Gone to see his *white* girl! [*They both laugh as at a joke.*]

FRIEND: Boy Teeka, how you does feel how your mother curry-favour him so much and doesn't even allow you to sit down in the car?

TEEKA: Oh, I sit down in it plenty times.

FRIEND: Only when you cleaning it! What I want to know is when you going to get a driving licence and drive it. That I have to see with my own eyes...

TEEKA: I don't bother with them and their stupid car... [*Sound of a car pulling up outside*] Wait! Talking about that, it sound as if Romesh come back! Peep over and see...

FRIEND: Yes... is Romesh... as if he had in a good few drinks, too, he fumbling to get out...

TEEKA: He don't usually come back so quick.

FRIEND: Well, I better go... I don't want him to catch me sitting here...

TEEKA: You stay right there, man! I invite you to have a drink with me, and nobody could put you out...

164

FRIEND: See if you could find out if is true they going to try out the harvester machine tomorrow. He should know.

[ROMESH *comes up. He has been drinking heavily...*]

ROMESH: Teeka?

TEEKA [*suddenly*]: What you want?

ROMESH: Who's home?

TEEKA: Just who you see... nobody else... your mother not here, if is she you mean.

ROMESH [*irritably*]: Just my damned luck! ...What's that you're having, rum?

TEEKA: Yes. But you don't want to drink with commoners like we, man... Your white friends don't drink rum?

ROMESH [*curtly*]: I'll get my own...

[*He goes inside and pours himself a drink.* TEEKA *and his* FRIEND *carry on an indistinct conversation... There is a chuckle or two... then they burst into loud laughter.* ROMESH *strides out, irrationally feeling that they are talking about him...*]

ROMESH: What's the big joke out here?

[*Teeka goes on laughing alone.*]

...It was something about me, wasn't it? I'll put you in your place. Damn you, Teeka.

[*He pushes aside the table spilling the drinks, and sends* TEEKA *sprawling against the wall. There is a dead silence for a moment or two...*]

ROMESH [*penitently*]: I'm sorry, Teeka. I don't know what came over me... I'm not myself, tonight... I... Let me help you up...

TEEKA [*with a note of finality*]: No!

FRIEND: We wasn't talking about you at all, Romesh. We was laughing about something that happen in the canefields this morning...

The next morning. The VILLAGERS *are gathered in a canefield to watch a demonstration of the harvest machine... There is a slight hubbub, not animated, but inclined to facetiousness and disbelief in the merits of the machine.*

HARRILAL: Now Pusher, don't stand in the front of the other men. What interest have you in the harvest machine, anyway?

PUSHER: Anything that happen in Wilderness is my business, Mr. Harrilal. You don't expect me to stay away from this demonstration what concern the workers in Wilderness.

HARRILAL: Well just keep to one side and don't obstruct the view for my men... Teeka, what you think of it?

TEEKA: It look like one of them space things they does send to the moon.

MAN ONE: You think it could cut cane, Mr. Harrilal?

HARRILAL: That's what we gather here to see... The Company send a white man to tell we about it. That's him shouting something now...

COMPANY MAN [at a distance]: Harrilal! You there in the crowd?

HARRILAL [shouting]: Yes sir!

COMPANY MAN: Are all the men here? Let the other villagers fall back and give them a chance.

HARRILAL [to crowd]: All right, keep quiet now and listen to what the man from the Company say... Keep back, Pusher, this don't concern you!

COMPANY MAN [addressing crowd]: Let's have some quiet now... [Silence falls.] ... Before the demonstration, are there any questions any of you would like to ask about the operating of the machine? [No reaction] No? Well, I know there is a fear among you that the machine will take away your jobs. But that is not true. We need men to operate and maintain it, and workers to clear the fields after the harvester has done its part. Also, not all the land is suitable for operating this machine, and it will be a long time before they come into general use. This demonstration is in the nature of an experiment really, but I am sure that when you see the harvester in action you will recognise what a boon it is to the whole sugar industry. In fact, already in Cuba and other parts of the world they have been using harvesters in the canefields for some time... You can all come a little closer... it won't bite you! No one wants to come forward to inspect it? [No reaction] ... What about you, Harrilal? Set an example to the men!

HARRILAL: We could see good from over here, sir...

COMPANY MAN: All right, if you say so. I tell you what. We'll leave

166

the harvester in Wilderness after the demonstration, and take it away tomorrow morning. That will give everyone a chance to examine it… At least become familiar with its appearance. Now pay attention, look closely and see how it works.

[*We hear the sound of the harvester starting up and going into action…. then fade…*]

Later in the village shop, there are animated arguments going on as the WORKERS *discuss the demonstration…*

MAN ONE: Lord, you see how it sweep through them cane in two-twos! No wonder every manjack run to the shop for a drink!

MAN TWO: And it does do the work of eighty-ninety men, think of that! I mean, one of them machines in Wilderness, and every villager out of work.

MAN ONE: That's it, it going to put everybody out of work, and we will all starve and suffer!

HARRILAL [*not liking the response, calls* TEEKA *to one side*]: Teeka! Come over here… listen. I don't like how the men arguing and drinking in the shop. They getting in a bad mood.

TEEKA: You expect them to have a celebration when you just see with your own eyes how that machine taking bread from their mouths?

HARRILAL: These things got to happen. I mean the Company got to modernise the industry… You hear what the Company man say about Cuba and them other countries…

TEEKA: You best hads explain that to them.

HARRILAL: No… I can't… I got to go out on something important, Teeka. I would of left your uncle Balgobin in charge, but I didn't see him at the demonstration.

TEEKA: He wasn't there, I was looking for him myself. And he not in the shop drinking either.

HARRILAL: Well you better take charge, Teeka. See that they don't drink too much… Try and get them back to work.

TEEKA: I not taking that responsibility. You can't see the mood they in?

HARRILAL: Well, do what you could… I really got some important business to attend to… If anybody ask for me just say you don't know which part I gone… I better slip out by the side door…

MAN ONE [*spotting* HARRILAL *sneaking out*]: Aye Harrilal! Where you going? Come here and explain what going to happen when this harvest machine take over, man!

HARRILAL [*as he goes*]: I will come back later... something important I just remember... Teeka will tell you about it... [*Fade out shop atmosphere.*]

In BALGOBIN's *hut later that evening...* POPO, *very excited about the harvester, arrives at the hut where* BALGOBIN *is ill and depressed.*

POPO [*coming up*]: Uncle! You seen the harvest machine? It look like a big invention!

BALGOBIN: Just leave the food and go, boy.

POPO: I went and seen it, Uncle! I went and sit down in the driver seat! Up there so high you could see the whole canefield! You ever sit down in the driver seat, Uncle?

BALGOBIN: I keep telling you, but like you would never learn, that when it come to cane, it ain't got nothing I don't know.

POPO: I think maybe now, instead of the cutlass, you could teach me to drive a harvester! Then you and me could do the work of eighty-ninety men!

BALGOBIN: You seen the machine working?

POPO: No-o, but they left it there in the fields.

BALGOBIN: Then how the hell you know it could do the work of eighty-ninety men?

POPO [*excitement cooling down*]: Everybody saying so... You don't believe?

BALGOBIN: What I know with my own brains, I don't need no blooming machine to teach me. It must of had men who cut that cane last night and stick them back in the ground to stand up, and then the machine pass over and fool people.

POPO: I hear Romesh say it will cut the work in half...

BALGOBIN: Aha! It doesn't only cut cane, it does cut work too! You listen to me, boy. Go in the hut and bring Poya out here. Let me show you how to really cut cane.

POPO [*hesitant*]: I... I can't stay now, Uncle... is full moon tonight, and I want to have another look at the machine.

BALGOBIN: So Poya not good enough for you now, eh? You rather go out and look at that monster what robbing honest people out of their living?

POPO [*edging away*]: You right, Uncle… It just like a monster… and I hear it can't go fast at all … and it breaking down all the time, so they have to have welders standing there to repair it… but I have to go now…

BALGOBIN: Wait boy! Let me show you…

POPO: Not now, Uncle… Tomorrow I will spend a long time with you… [*He leaves, embarrassed.*]

In the rumshop, later that night. BALGOBIN *is the last one remaining.*

SOUZA [*long yawn*]: Ah-h-h… Aye, Balgobin! You can't see everybody gone home to sleep, man? Is time to shut the shop.

BALGOBIN: I just finishing this drink.

SOUZA: Well hurry up. All this harvester confusion in Wilderness got me confuse and tired… Praise God I don't have to cut cane for a living…

[BALGOBIN *leaves after finishing his drink. He heads towards the machine. The tone of the monologue in this scene contrasts: it is soft and affectionate when addressing Poya, raging and frustrated when talking to the harvester.*]

BALGOBIN [*to Poya*]: Poya my friend, we got a job to do tonight… it might be the last job we ever do, so we got to do it good good… You and me, Poya, we been all over Trinidad together, right? We work in Orange Valley, La Gloria, Cross Crossing… it ain't have no cane estate we ain't work on, right? And our Destiny bring us to Wilderness, so we could do this last job here tonight, and save all the poor people in the village who got to have work, else how they going to buy bread to keep alive? Ah, we getting nearer, Poya! Look at it over there in the moonlight, a juggernauth of destruction, come to cause misery and woe to peaceful people… We best approach quiet, in case they have watchman put out to keep guard… We make a little circle so… and come up from behind… [*To machine now, shouting*] All right! Come on out! One by one! Or the whole eighty-ninety of you at one time! I don't care how you come, me and Poya will chop every manjack down like how you chop the cane! [*Short silence, then he chuckles to Poya*] Poya, look at all them scamps and cowards, they so 'fraid they playing as if they sleeping!

169

[*There is a dull metallic thud as he beats the side of the harvester with his hand…*]

[*To machine*] …Come on, wake up in there! All-you come to take away my work, eh? Come on, we have a fair fight, is only Balgobin and Poya waiting out here. If you win is because I dead. And when you lose is because every one of you is laying down like cane when Poya pass like a sword of vengeance… [*Voice rising to a scream*] All you frighten of one man? [*Fit of coughing*] …Don't let that cough fool you and think you is facing a sick old man… I don't want any excuses… This is me, Balgobin the great, and my trusty friend Poya, who live by the sweat of the brow… [*Silence… Then to Poya*] …Maybe they ganging up on the other side, getting ready to make a rush… Let we go and see… [*As he moves,* BALGOBIN *stumps his toe on a caneroot.*] …Blasted thing! I stump my toe on a caneroot! [*To machine*] That is the way you reap cane? Leaving a big stump in the ground to break men foot? It look like I will have to give you all a lesson here tonight in the art of the cane cutter… [*To Poya*] … They want we to show them how to do the work, Poya. Come. Look, some cane standing there… [*He moves to a patch of cane and begins to cut with swift efficiency.*] … Like this… and this… me and Poya better than any machine… h'mm some of these cane tough! I wonder if is those rascals who creep up on me when my back turn, and pretending they is cane? [*To Poya*] Look, Poya, they surround we when we wasn't looking! Come on, we only got about eighty of them to slaughter! [BALGOBIN *attacks the 'men' with renewed fury, slashing wildly left and right. He addresses the machine*] …That's the way you-all want to fight, eh? One… two… three… four… five… [*Fade on his final counting, which gets a little slower, with gasps for breath…*] …eighty-six, eighty-seven, eighty-eight… [*He stops and laughs deeply in triumph. The laugh turns into a heavy fit of coughing. He recovers… He addresses the machine*] …Any more? Maybe it got some of you still hiding in there inside the machine… [*To Poya*] Come Poya, let we attack them at home, and slaughter whatever cowards remaining… [*He starts to clamber up the machine, breathing hard and panting with exertion. He reaches the top.*] …All right, Poya, we standing on top the monster now. Just one big stroke, Poya, and we will slice him in half. Like this. [*There is a whining ring of steel as he brings down the cutlass in a tremendous stroke. The jolt flings the cutlass from his grasp and it falls with a clatter on the harvester and* BALGOBIN *himself stumbles and falls.*] …Oho! So they set a trap after all! First time in my life that Poya ever meet with resistance, and even make me drop him down and fall myself! Well, when you fall is only one thing to do… get up… [*He gets up.*] H'mm … this thing here by my foot feel like some oil connection leaking. That's why I slip and fall! [*To Poya*] Right, Poya, we discover their soft spot! We still going to win the battle, all we have to do is strike a match and burn them out of their nest…

[*He strikes a match… then another and sets the harvester on fire. The flames crackle and spread quickly into a roaring inferno. The sound of the burning continues for a few seconds and then fades…*]

Next morning, SEETA *and* ROMESH *are at breakfast.* SEETA *is trying to bridge the gap widening between them.*

SEETA: You hardly eating a thing, Romesh, and I make this breakfast especially this morning.

ROMESH [*brusquely*]: I'm not hungry.

SEETA: You got to keep your strength up you know… Try some more of those fresh tomatoes… You want me to slice them up? I only left them whole because I know you like to have them that way.

ROMESH: Just leave me alone…

SEETA: My! These days you really getting touch-ous… You just dashing in from work and dashing out again… We don't have any nice chats like we used to…

ROMESH: I don't remember any. Besides, has it occurred to you that maybe I have nothing to say?

SEETA: I know you got something on your mind. You been brooding and sulking like when you was a little boy, and avoiding me. Why?

ROMESH: Maybe I see too much of you.

SEETA: You full of 'maybes' this morning… I don't see enough of you. If anything disturbing you, Romesh, you should tell me… That's what a mother is for…

[ROMESH *makes a grunting sound.*]

171

SEETA: Come on, tell me what it is, I don't like to see you looking so miserable... You had a quarrel with Petra?

ROMESH: Just keep her name out of it... You're talking to yourself, you know. I'm not listening to a word you're saying.

SEETA [*persisting*]: What is it then, something with the job? You not getting along with the Company? Because, if that, I can go along and have a talk with them...

ROMESH: Look, if you knew what you were doing, you'd just keep quiet and keep away from me.

SEETA: Something wrong, and I got to find out what.

ROMESH [*grimly*]: Don't fret yourself. I am going to pack and get out of Wilderness. All you're doing is hastening the day.

SEETA [*disbelieving*]: Pack and get out! You making joke so early in the morning!

ROMESH [*with emotional control*]: This one is no joke, believe me. I feel I'm going to explode if I stay any longer... You've done your best to make me miserable, and I can't take any more...

SEETA [*sniffing*]: I can't seem to do anything right for you... and I try my best...

ROMESH: All you do is interfere.

SEETA: Like what so, Romesh? Mention a few things!

ROMESH: I won't know where to start... Perhaps in your womb, before I was born.

SEETA: If it's the politics that upset you... Maybe Petra don't like the idea...

ROMESH: Call her name once more, and I'll walk out this instant!

SEETA: All right, all right. Don't shout at me Romesh... [*Sniff*] If it make you happy, I could drop the whole thing...

ROMESH: I don't care what you drop. I'm suffering in this house. You even object to my having a drink with my friends in the shop... not that I've got any left...

SEETA: You know why... That sort of thing is for Teeka and Harrilal, not you... That's why I stock up the house with so much drink... You go in the shop and start making jokes with the villagers, and they lose all respect for you...

ROMESH: Then there's the big mystery about my Uncle Balgobin. Why mustn't I see him? Why can't he come to the house? I've half a mind to go and see him this very morning!

SEETA: No no, Romesh! You promise me you won't!

ROMESH [*dry laugh*]: Promise...

SEETA: Yes, you promise me already, and you never break a promise to me... He not good for you, he will only drag you down to his level...

ROMESH: Oh well... all that isn't important any more. I'll soon be away from here.

SEETA [*from sniffing to quiet sobs now*]: I don't know what I do to you, Romesh... You never treat me like this before...

ROMESH [*upset by her crying*]: Stop that silly crying. It won't help matters.

SEETA [*louder sobbing*]: You know how much I love you... I make so many sacrifices for you... Come and hold my hand...

ROMESH [*quickly*]: No! I'd better go to work now...

SEETA: Just sit here next to me a little before you go... Let me stroke your hair... You can't leave me like this, Romesh...

ROMESH [*weakening*]: I ... I'll be late for work... and I don't want to come too near to you...

[*There is a shout from outside, breaking the mood...* PUSHER *has discovered the wrecked harvester on his morning rounds.*]

PUSHER [*distant shout*]: Mr. Harrilal! Mr. Harrilal!

ROMESH: Who is it?

SEETA [*recovering quickly*]: Must be somebody looking for him... and he gone to the shop. Just ignore it...

PUSHER [*nearer*]: Mr. Harrilal! Disaster! The world come to an end!

SEETA: It sound like Pusher... I better see what it's about... [*She moves to the gallery... To* PUSHER] What you want, Pusher?

PUSHER [*in great excitement, shouting*]: Miss Seeta! Get Mr. Harrilal quick!

SEETA: He not here. What happen?

PUSHER: The whole harvester burn down!

SEETA: What nonsense you talking about?

PUSHER: I seen it! I was just making my rounds, Miss Seeta... you know how I got to look after Wilderness... and I seen it in the fields... It burn right down to the ground...

Later in the shop, that morning. There is an excited atmosphere. The news has brought a wave of newspaper men, T.V. cameras and police... There is a great hubbub in the shop... It is sustained unless indicated... These asides are picked up...

173

MAN ONE: You see what happening in Trinidad now? The workers will unite and create a big revolution if they don't get their rights!

MAN TWO: And whoever destroy that harvester will go down in history as the saviour of the working masses!

REPORTER [*going up to* HARRILAL]: Excuse me... Are you Mr. Harrilal?

HARRILAL: Yes?

REPORTER: I represent the *Guardian* ...I would like to interview you away from all this...

HARRILAL: I got no statement to make unless you got permission from the Company... I not talking to a soul.

REPORTER: When did it happen? Who discovered it?

HARRILAL: See if you find a fellar name Pusher in all that crowd... he was the first one...

REPORTER: Thanks... [*Starts looking for* PUSHER *in the crowd...*] ...Mr. Pusher... I'm looking for Mr. Pusher...

PUSHER: You calling my name, mister?

REPORTER: Mr. Pusher?

PUSHER: That's right.

REPORTER: You were the first man to see the harvester... what's left of it?

PUSHER: Who else but me, who look after the whole village, making my rounds day after day faithfully?

REPORTER: Would you tell me the story?... Let's go outside, I can't hear myself in this shop...

[PUSHER *and the* REPORTER *move outside where the background noise is quieter.* PUSHER *has never had it so good and intends to get the most out of the situation.*]

PUSHER: Right, we outside now... First thing I want to know is, I going to get my photo in the papers? I seen a lot of cameras about... You represent T.V.?

REPORTER: Not really...

PUSHER: We never seen a television in Wilderness before... They going to make a film?

REPORTER: Just tell me what time it was...

PUSHER: Before you start, we best hads get one thing clear. I mean, it got so many of you fellars here from Port of Spain, and even further parts... Why I should talk to you and nobody else? You can't organise a press conference? People in Wilderness not stupid, you know!

174

REPORTER: I just want you to answer a few questions…

PUSHER: I hear you fellars does pay a fee for information. How much you paying?

REPORTER [*embarrassed laugh*]: …You going to get your photo BIG in the papers, man… What more do you want?

PUSHER: You think I fall off a tree? I will talk to the newspaper what paying the most… It ain't got another man know as much about Wilderness and what happening here as me… born and bred in the canefields…

REPORTER: Well… maybe we can arrange a fee… Now, what's your full name?

PUSHER: Pusher. Just Pusher, like the boss who push the work, right? …It must of happen last night, you know… and this morning, when I was making my rounds… I got to make sure things all right in the village, you see, so I make my rounds two or three times a day… This morning when I look across by the canefield where the harvester was, I notice something wrong…

In Port of Spain in the offices of the Company, MR. FORBES *is listening to the latest cricket news…*

COMMENTATOR: …perhaps the ball did turn a bit, but the fact remains that it is now a tense situation with that crucial wicket down… The West Indians have been hoping for this, and it is only a question of time now…

[*There is a knock at the door and* ROMESH *comes in…*]

FORBES [*switching off the radio*]: Come in Romesh…

ROMESH: You sent for me?

FORBES: Yes. Sit down… Those reporters still hanging around outside?

ROMESH: Yes. And more arriving.

FORBES: You haven't been talking to any of them have you?

ROMESH: Me? Why, no?

FORBES: I just thought as the harvester was destroyed on your father's estate in Wilderness… some bright chap might want to interview you…

ROMESH: What I know is common knowledge… I've no more idea about what happened than you.

FORBES: This is a bad business… There's labour unrest all over the island, and it only needs something like this to spark off trouble among the caneworkers. What was it like in Wilderness? How did they take it?

ROMESH: I suppose they didn't like the idea from the beginning… I told my father to explain that these technical improvements would benefit the whole industry in the end… I didn't see anybody in the fields when I was coming to work this morning… I usually take a short cut, off the main road, and pass some of them on the way…

FORBES: The damage is done, but the Company can't afford to leave the matter like that. We've got to find out who did it… I saw a report a little while ago. It seems as if someone ran amok with a cutlass or something and literally tried to destroy the machine with it before setting it on fire…

ROMESH: That's more than I know…

FORBES: Do you know the men in the village well?

ROMESH: No. I used to, at one time… but not any more.

FORBES: We've got to find out who did it… I wanted to see you because I thought you might have some idea, seeing that it happened on your doorstep so to speak…

ROMESH: Isn't it a job for some other department of the Company?

FORBES: You don't think I begged for this? The fact is, you happen to belong to my section… You live in Wilderness…

ROMESH: I don't move around… I might as well be in town.

FORBES: But perhaps if you did, you might get a clue? The villagers would be more likely to talk to you than to the horde of reporters and investigators who are swarming all over. Our own man says he is in a hopeless situation…

ROMESH [*dry laugh*]: You mean for me to play detective?

FORBES: It won't do for this affair to linger on… It won't do the Company any good… Reports have been coming in that some of the other estates have stopped work…

ROMESH: But what do you expect of me? I don't think I could find out anything.

FORBES: You can keep your eyes and your ears open, anyway. It's only a suggestion… If you feel you're in sympathy with the village…

ROMESH: It isn't that. It's just that all this doesn't really affect me. I'd rather stay out of it completely. I'm leaving Wilderness, anyway, and going to live in town.

FORBES: Well, anything you can find out might help us. The Company is offering a reward for information of any sort that would assist our investigator. Keep it in mind, just in case you happen to hear or see anything... [*Fade out*]

Outside BALGOBIN's *hut that evening.* POPO *is visiting his uncle, who is very ill. The boy is wildly excited about what is happening in the village...*

POPO [*approaching*]: Uncle! Uncle!

BALGOBIN [*weakly, resting in his hut*]: Come inside boy... I laying down...

POPO [*entering hut*]: What happen Uncle, you feeling sick?

BALGOBIN: I just resting here on the mattress in the corner...

POPO: You better eat the food while it hot...

BALGOBIN: I not hungry... Just rest it there on the table...

POPO [*crestfallen*]: All right... I thought you might of wanted to hear what happening in the village... So much excitement...

BALGOBIN: I know you wouldn't go until you spread your gossip. Talk quick and go!

POPO: Everybody talking about Pusher! He is the main subject of conversation!

BALGOBIN: What happen, the old scamp dead at last?

POPO: No. He say that is he who lick-up and mash-up the harvester machine!

BALGOBIN [*starting to laugh, which turns to coughing, then gasping*]: Push... Pusher?

POPO: But nobody believe him. Is a big joke. We even give him a new name ... 'Combine'.

BALGOBIN: Combine?

POPO: Yes, that's what they call the harvester, Combine.

BALGOBIN: Oh... [*Musing*] That old son of a bitch was always after fame and glory, even if he got to thief it from somebody else!

POPO: He got the detectives on him though, because the Company want quick action, and they have to accuse somebody...

BALGOBIN: Well, they 'cusing the wrong man, I could tell you.

POPO: Who did it, Uncle? Who is the real criminal? You bound to know, as you know everything!

BALGOBIN: Sure I know. How many times I got to tell you...

POPO [*interrupting*]: Who it was then? They offering BIG reward for information!

BALGOBIN: Well you could collect that reward, Popo. You really want to know?

POPO: Yes, yes!

BALGOBIN: Then bring Poya from the corner there, near to the lamp where you could see...

POPO [*goes and gets the cutlass and is surprised and dismayed at its condition*]: Uncle! What happen to the cutlass? The blade all jagged-up and twist!

BALGOBIN [*a little dramatic now and proud*]: That's who destroy the monster, Popo. Poya. Even though it cost him his life, and he would never be able to cut cane again... And naturally, I help him a little...

POPO [*brief silence, in awe*]: You! You, Uncle?

BALGOBIN: Who else you think? The people of Trinidad always forming committees, and having conferences, and arsing around when they have any problems. The way to treat a problem is to tackle it right away and chop off the head. That's what Poya and me do.

POPO: You mean, you *one* did it?

BALGOBIN: And Poya. Don't forget Poya!

POPO: Tell me how you do it. Please Uncle. Please...

BALGOBIN [*livening up*]: Well... just let me raise off this mattress... [*He gets up.*] ...Hand me Poya... Now watch... It was like this you see. The two of we creep up on them in the moonlight... [*His voice is full of strength to begin with.*] ...It must of had about three-four hundred of the rascals hiding in the monster belly but it was no difference to me if it had a million...

[*Fade out and fade up the end of the story, his voice now tired and weak...*]

BALGOBIN: ...and that's the way it happen, Popo. One las' battle what cost me and Poya our lives, because it look if me too seeing my last days... [*Heavy fit of coughing*]

POPO [*in a disappointed tone*]: You could of told me you was going... I could of been your spy, I could of help you to fight them, and you wouldn't of had to mash up poor Poya so much!

BALGOBIN: You would of only get in trouble, boy... I better go back and lay down... [*He retires to bed.*]

POPO: What trouble? [*Then he realises.*] Uncle, suppose they catch you?

BALGOBIN: They would have to work fast to beat Death.

POPO [*concerned*]: You better go away from Wilderness! You better go to one of the estates down South, where they can't find you!

BALGOBIN [*tiredly*]: I just want to sleep…

POPO: But Uncle! They will lock you up in jail! What you going to do?

BALGOBIN: Just sleep… I feeling so tired as if I could sleep and don't bother to get up again… [*Fade*]

A little later at HARRILAL's *and* SEETA's *house.* ROMESH *is about to drive away in his car to town when* POPO *comes running to him.* ROMESH *keeps the engine running throughout their dialogue…*

POPO [*coming up*]: Romesh! You going out?

ROMESH: Yes… You should be in bed, Popo.

POPO: Uncle in big trouble, Romesh!

ROMESH: Oh? What's he done?

POPO: You promise you won't tell nobody?

ROMESH: Promise.

POPO: Well, he went, he-one, and lick-up the harvester and set it on fire!

ROMESH [*humouring* POPO]: Oh! I thought Pusher was the one?

POPO: No! No! It was Uncle! Uncle and Poya!

ROMESH: O-oh! Somebody helped him, eh?

POPO: Poya is his cutlass.

ROMESH: I see… Well, you can get your reward, Popo. Just run down a road and tell a policeman.

POPO: I don't want no stupid reward! I just want to save Uncle Balgobin! You don't believe, Romesh? Uncle tell me himself, and show me the cutlass, all jagged-up and broken.

ROMESH: Yes… well, I've got to go to town, I'll be late…

POPO [*bitterly*]: If *you* don't believe me, who would?

ROMESH: I tell you what. You look for your father and tell him. He'd know what to do.

POPO: I don't see him anywhere.

ROMESH: He'll be home soon.

POPO [*doubtful*]: You think I should?

ROMESH: Sure, he's your father, he knows what's best… Move away now, I've got to go… [ROMESH *revs up and drives off.*]

The next morning. SEETA *is in the kitchen. She notices a figure huddled on the back steps. It is* BALGOBIN…

SEETA [*to sounds of washing-up*]: Who is that sitting on my back step this morning? [*Calls*] That you, Pusher? [BALGOBIN *coughs deeply.*] …Who is it? [*Doubtful*] …Pusher?… [*She goes down the wooden steps.*] …You! How dare you come to my house! Go away at once! I don't want to set eyes on you! You lucky nobody here, else I get them to beat you and chase you out of my yard!

BALGOBIN [*weakly*]: Seeta… Seeta… I sick too bad…

SEETA: I don't care if you dying! Go and dead somewhere else!

BALGOBIN: I… I don't think I could move… I use up my last strength getting here…

SEETA [*scoffing*]: Sick! I don't doubt! You should of dead years ago!

BALGOBIN: I … can't move, Seeta.

SEETA [*reluctant concern*]: H'm… like you really sick bad…

BALGOBIN: One thing I got to say… It was me who burn down the harvester…

SEETA: You sick in truth… You going off your head and talking rubbish… Come, I suppose I better let you sit inside a little…

BALGOBIN: I… I can't raise up…

SEETA: Let me help you… Put your weight on me, not that stupid cutlass you still carrying around! [*She helps him into the house.*]

BALGOBIN: Look… See the cutlass, how it bend-up…

SEETA: Hush, don't talk… I better put you in Romesh room to lay down on the bed a little. Come… [*She takes him to the bedroom and helps him onto the bed, patting the pillow and smoothing the sheet.*] …You lay down there. You will feel better and then you can go.

BALGOBIN: But Seeta… I got to tell you…

SEETA: Keep quiet. I will go and make you a cup of tea… Your face hot like fire…

BALGOBIN [*summoning strength*]: I won't keep quiet till you listen to what I have to say.

SEETA [*sighing*]: Ah… you still as stubborn as ever, Balgo… What it is?

BALGOBIN: The harvester. Is I who mash it up. I not lying… You can't see how the cutlass mash-up?

SEETA [*with a pause, as she takes this in*]: O God! You realise what you saying?

180

BALGOBIN: Yes.

SEETA: Confusion follow wherever you go. You bring all your bad luck with you to Wilderness... You don't know what this mean!

BALGOBIN: I sorry, Seeta, but...

SEETA: Wait, let me think! Who else know about this?

BALGOBIN: I only tell Popo... but he must of told Harrilal, because I hear he was looking for me... I don't know if he tell the police...

SEETA: Worse and worse! Oh lord, what a mess you put me in, Balgo! Listen... you got to stay here. Nobody would look for you in this house.

BALGOBIN: Whatever you say. I...

SEETA: Now you hear what I got to say. You dream that it was you, that's all. It was Pusher who done it. You hear?

BALGOBIN: No, it was me...

SEETA: Pusher, Pusher, PUSHER! Everybody in Wilderness know it was him. You say after me. Pusher...

BALGOBIN: I ... I tired, Seeta.

SEETA [*relentless*]: Say it! Say Pusher burn the harvester.

BALGOBIN: Yes... whatever you say... Pusher... harvester Pusher... [*His voice grows weak and fades...*]

[*A little later* PUSHER *is summoned to the house...*]

PUSHER: You send for me Miss Seeta?

SEETA: Yes, Pusher... Come inside the kitchen ... Sit down... You want a drink?

PUSHER [*quickly*]: Yes! [*Delayed surprise*] A drink?

SEETA: Yes [*She pours a liberal shot.*] ...Here. Wet your throat.

PUSHER: Thanks... [*Takes a long swig*] ...A-ah, I been talking so much to the reporters, I was really thirsty...

SEETA: So I hear, Pusher... and the fools don't believe you had enough guts to burn down the harvester, eh?

PUSHER: I tell them over and over... Now they concocting a new story. Mr. Harrilal telling everybody that your son Romesh report to the company that is Balgobin who do it.

SEETA: Lies, Pusher, all lies. They trying to take away the glory and fame from you... Have another drink... [*She pours again.*]

PUSHER: The trouble is, they won't believe.

SEETA: But I believe you, Pusher! I believe you was brave enough to sacrifice yourself for the working classes... You know, before this business finish, they might put up a statue of you in Independence Square in Port of Spain! You will become famous, a hero!

PUSHER: I had a interview... They going to put my photo in the papers...

SEETA: You just stick to your story. Don't let anybody put you off.

PUSHER: The thing is, they say I can't substantiate my story.

SEETA: I have that for you. Here... this is the cutlass you use... [*Gives him* BALGOBIN's *cutlass*]

PUSHER: Aha! And look how it break up in truth, when I was fighting the harvester!

SEETA: Exactly. You know it's your business to look after Wilderness, that's why you couldn't bear to see no machine take away jobs from the villagers.

PUSHER: Yes, and me, Pusher, who everybody think old and stupid, save the whole village.

SEETA: You take that cutlass and show the police. They will bound to believe you. But don't tell them where you get it from! You understand that?

PUSHER: I didn't fall off no tree, you know Miss Seeta. I know you don't want your name mix up in all this business.

SEETA: Good. Don't forget! If they still don't believe, I will come to your rescue and say that I seen you going out there that night myself.

PUSHER: Well! That is substantiation! If you say so, they have to listen!

SEETA: And not a single word about coming here and talking to me. If any questions, just say I wanted you to cut the grass in the yard. You understand?

PUSHER: Yes... Another drink would make me understand better yet.

SEETA: No. Don't drink here. Look... [*Takes money*] Take this money.

PUSHER: Money too!

SEETA: Yes. You never have any, and if they catch you with so much on you, it will help substantiate your story. When you get to the shop, start buying drinks for everybody, and in no time at all the police will be asking you where you got it... Then what you going to say?

PUSHER: I going to say that I get it for burning down the harvester? I not stupid to say you give me!

SEETA: Well... yes. That'll put them off... Tell them some trade union man that you can't remember give you a bribe... It got so much confusion in Trinidad now that that is the sort of thing they expecting... [Fade]

Later that evening, PETRA has come to Wilderness after a phone call from SEETA... From this scene to the end of the play, SEETA is a different woman, broken, distraught...

PETRA [calling]: Hello! Anybody home? Seeta?

SEETA [coming to the front]: Petra! I too glad to see you... Come inside and sit down... You get here all right?

PETRA: Yes... but there seems to be a lot of confusion in the village... crowds of people about... What's happening? You sounded so distressed on the phone.

SEETA: I don't know where to begin... You want a drink?

PETRA: Thank you... Better have one yourself, you're shaking.

SEETA: Yes... some brandy.

PETRA: It's all in the news about the trouble here... Romesh still at work?

SEETA [back with the drinks]: He doesn't come until later... That's why I ask you to try and get here quick.

PETRA [sipping drink]: What's going on then?

SEETA: When I tell you, you mustn't hold anything against me. All I done, all my life, was for Romesh. You believe that?

PETRA: I suppose so.

SEETA: Romesh will be my judge... Remind him how much I love him, Petra... I know the both of you planning for him to leave Wilderness...

PETRA: Now, Seeta, I don't make decisions for Romesh. You do enough of that for him...

SEETA: You better hear what I have to say... You know that Balgobin and Harrilal is brothers... When I was small, my parents arrange my marriage. But it was Balgobin I was in love with... [Her voice grows soft, musing, showing a new aspect to her character.] ...You might think I don't know what love is, Petra... but it was the happiest time of my life... We had some good times together, Balgo and me... [Sighs, and then changes tone] Ah well, you never

183

miss the water till the well runs dry, as the old calypso say… To cut a long story short, what I leading up to is that Balgobin is really Romesh father…

PETRA: Oh!

SEETA: Nobody know excepting you. Not even Balgobin.

PETRA: And Romesh?

SEETA: Least of all. You think I wanted him to grow up knowing he was a bastard? That his father was a shiftless drunken vagabond drifting from sugar estate to sugar estate all over the island?

PETRA [*with a pause*]: So… you substituted Romesh for his father?

SEETA: No! I love Romesh. I hate Balgobin… I mean… Oh, this trouble have my head spinning… I don't know where to turn! You got to help me, Petra. I got no-one; even Romesh turn against me these days.

PETRA: You've got Harrilal.

SEETA: Him! He so coward and weak that he must clear off out of the village, afraid to face the men! And before he went he spread the story that it was Romesh who inform the Company that Balgobin responsible for destroying the harvester.

PETRA: Is that true? Did Balgobin do it?

SEETA [*beginning to sob*]: I don't know… it's just like him to do a thing like that… Listen! What's that?

[*The noise of an angry crowd comes into the house. The workers are congregating in the street outside… There are angry shouts…*]

PETRA: Sounds like some disturbance in the street…

SEETA: Is Teeka! I sure he stirring up the workers to cause trouble! Oh, I wish Romesh come home soon! I got Balgobin hiding here.

PETRA [*alarmed*]: You have him in the house?

SEETA: Yes… He so sick he can't move. This morning I find him on the backsteps…

[*A little later, we hear the aggressive sounds of the crowd as* ROMESH *gets through and enters the house…*]

ROMESH: Petra! What're you doing here?

SEETA: I… I send for she, Romesh… I too glad you come!

PETRA: It's all right, Romesh… calm down… Let me get you a drink.

ROMESH [*to* SEETA]: You brought her here in all this trouble? You realise there's a mob out there itching to start something?

PETRA [*aside to* ROMESH]: Leave Seeta alone, Romesh... Can't you see what a state she's in? ... [*Bringing drinks*] ...Here sit down and drink this... and you'd better have another brandy, Seeta.

SEETA [*sobbing quietly*]: I... I don't want no more... You tell him, Petra, tell him everything, the whole story, don't hold nothing back...

[*Fade, then fade up on* PETRA *finishing the story...*]

PETRA: So you must understand. I know it's a lot to take in at once.

ROMESH [*with a pause, very quietly*]: He's here? In my room?

PETRA: Yes... he's very ill, Romesh. I don't think he's conscious...

[ROMESH *walks slowly to his room, opens the door, goes in and shuts it behind him.*]

SEETA: He going to dead, Petra, Balgo going to dead!

PETRA: Try and pull yourself together... Think of what we're going to do now.

SEETA: Do? I got no hope left... for anything... I don't care any more... I wish I could dead with Balgo.

PETRA [*sharply*]: Stop talking nonsense! Maybe if we could get a doctor...

SEETA: It's no use... is just as if the whole thing was planned to happen like how it happening...

[*Outside, the noise from the crowd grows more threatening. There is a shout from* TEEKA...]

TEEKA [*shouting*]: Aye, Mr. Big-Shot Romesh! We want Balgobin. We know you got him inside the house!

SEETA [*moving to the gallery*]: Let me talk to them... [*Shouts*] Teeka! It wasn't Romesh! It was your own father Harrilal who tell the Company!

TEEKA [*backed by jeers from the crowd*]: You always stick up for Romesh! But you can't save him now!

SEETA [*returning to* PETRA]: They wouldn't listen... I hope Teeka could control them...

[*The bedroom door opens and* ROMESH *comes out slowly...*]

SEETA: Romesh, my son!

PETRA [*sharply*]: Leave him alone, Seeta!

SEETA: I... I only wanted to touch him... [*She sits down and sobs quietly.*]

ROMESH [*as if in a daze*]: Petra.

PETRA [*gently*]: Romesh.

ROMESH: I think he's dead... and... and I never got a chance to speak to him.

PETRA: But he came home in the end.

ROMESH: Did she tell him about me?

PETRA: I don't know... but I did. He was conscious for a minute while I was in there...

ROMESH: You had more than me... Did he understand?

PETRA: I'm... not sure.

ROMESH: Well, it makes no difference now...

PETRA: Would you like something... coffee? A drink?

ROMESH: No.

SEETA [*mourning*]: Romesh, Romesh, what we going to do now?

ROMESH: I'm going out to them.

PETRA: You think you should?

SEETA: No, no, Romesh! Stop him Petra! They will kill him too.

[*But* ROMESH *is already outside... The mob greets him with jeers and shouts...*]

MAN ONE: White Indian!

MAN TWO: You send your own Uncle to jail!

ROMESH [*above noise, to* TEEKA]: Teeka, tell them they're only making it worse for themselves. My fath... Balgobin is dead...

TEEKA [*screeching*]: You kill him!

MAN THREE: We should stone him out of Wilderness!

MAN TWO: Chase him and his white woman out of the village!

[*The mob reacts to the news and a stone is flung and crashes against the house...*]

TEEKA: No, wait! Don't touch him! Don't do anything to him! That is what he want... But he will have to suffer more if we do nothing!

[*As* PETRA *comes out the mob quieten down a little...*]

MAN THREE: Aha! Look the white woman coming!

MAN TWO: Take care she not some Company Director daughter!

ROMESH [*urgently*]: Petra! Keep away from here! Get back quickly!

TEEKA [*stirring mob*]: What happen to you-all? You just got to see a white face and you-all ready to run? Them days finish! We got independence now, and white man got no more rule! Black Power is King now!

ROMESH: I'll kill you if anything happens to her, Teeka!

TEEKA [*jeering*]: Don't worry, I won't even give you that satisfaction... [*To crowd*] Leave she alone too, don't interfere! Just chuck the two of them in the car and let them go!

PETRA [*sharply, as someone moves towards her*]: Don't you dare touch me! We'll go for ourselves. Come, Romesh.

ROMESH [*hesitant*]: Seeta.

PETRA: They won't harm *her*... Let's get away from here...

> [*They get into the car. She starts the engine... The mob beat at the body of the car and make a great clamour.* PETRA *toots the horn several times... As they get to the edge of the crowd she accelerates and they drive off. The sounds of the mob fade away, then the car itself...*]

Two days later, at BALGOBIN's *funeral on the banks of the Caroni River. The crackling logs of the funeral pyre can be heard. Then fade to a background and* ROMESH *and* PETRA *viewing the scene from a distant bridge near the road...*

ROMESH: This is the sort of funeral Balgobin would have liked, his ashes cast on the river flowing through the canefields...

PETRA: Would you like to go nearer?

ROMESH: No, we'll stay here on the bridge...

PETRA: I think that's Seeta, in the purple sari... Hard to tell from this distance.

ROMESH: Yes, it's her.

PETRA [*with a pause*]: What's going to happen with us, Romesh?

ROMESH: I'll be going to England soon...

PETRA: ...and coming back?

ROMESH: Do you want me to?

PETRA: You know what I want... but it will have to be definite. I'll wait for you, but don't return with any more doubts.

ROMESH: I can promise you that, if nothing else… Let's go.

PETRA: Don't you want to stay until it's finished?

ROMESH: It finished when he died… those flames on the pyre are only symbolic… I'd rather leave now. Come…

[*They enter the car and drive off. The sounds of the funeral pyre are all that can be heard.*]

THE END

TRINIDADIAN BOOKS FROM PEEPAL TREE PRESS

www.peepaltreepress.com

James C. Aboud	*Lagahoo Poems*	£7.99
Kevyn Alan Arthur	*The View from Belmont*	£8.99
Laurence A. Breiner	*Black Yeats*	£16.99
Mark De Brito	*Heron's Canoe*	£7.99
Brenda Flanagan	*You Alone are Dancing*	£7.99
Anson Gonzalez	*Crossroads of Dream*	£7.99
Anson Gonzalez	*Collected Poems*	£8.99
Vishnu Gosine	*The Coming of Lights*	£7.99
Cecil Gray	*The Woolgatherer*	£8.99
Ismith Khan	*The Crucifixion*	£7.99
Ismith Khan	*A Day in the Country*	£8.99
Rabindranath Maharaj	*The Writer and his Wife*	£8.99
L. Manoo-Rahming	*Curry Flavour*	£7.99
marina maxwell	*Decades to Ama*	£9.99
marina maxwell	*Chopstix in Mauby*	£8.99
Sharlow Mohammed	*The Elect*	£7.99
Lakshmi Persaud	*Sastra*	£9.99
Lakshmi Persaud	*Butterfly In The Wind*	£7.99
Jennifer Rahim	*Between The Fence And The Forest*	£7.99
Jennifer Rahim	*Songster and Other Stories*	£8.99
Raymond Ramcharitar	*American Fall*	£7.99
Eric Merton Roach	*The Flowering Rock*	£9.99
Sam Selvon	*Highway in the Sun*	£8.99
Sam Selvon	*Eldorado West One*	£7.99
Martin Zehnder	*Something Rich and Strange:*	
	Selected Essays on Samuel Selvon	£14.99

JENNIFER RAHIM

Songster and Other Stories

Rahim's stories move between the present and the past to make sense of the tensions between image and reality in contemporary Trinidad. The contemporary stories show the traditional, communal world in retreat before the forces of local and global capitalism. A popular local fisherman is gunned down when he challenges the closure of the beach for a private club catering to white visitors and the new elite; the internet becomes a rare safe place for an AIDS sufferer to articulate her pain; cocaine has become the scourge even of the rural communities. But the stories set thirty years earlier in the narrating 'I's' childhood reveal that the 'old-time' Trinidad was already breaking up. The old pieties about nature symbolised by belief in the presence of the folk-figure of 'Papa Bois' are powerless to prevent the ruthless plunder of the forests; communal stability has already been uprooted by the pulls towards emigration, and any sense that Trinidad was ever edenic is undermined by images of the destructive power of alcohol and the casual presence of paedophilic sexual abuse.

Rahim's Trinidad, is though, as her final story makes clear, the creation of a writer who has chosen to stay, and she is highly conscious that her perspective is very different from those who have taken home away in a suitcase, or who visit once a year. Her Trinidad is 'not a world in my head like a fantasy', but the island that 'lives and moves in the bloodstream'. Her reflection on the nature of small island life is as fierce and perceptive as Jamaica Kincaid's *A Small Place*, but comes from and arrives at a quite opposite place. What Rahim finds in her island is a certain existential insouciance and the capacity of its people, whatever their material circumstance, to commit to life in the knowledge of its bitter-sweetness.

ISBN 13:9781845230487
UKList price: £8.99 US$19.95 CAN$24.95

NEW 2007

LAURENCE A. BREINER
Black Yeats: Eric Roach and the Politics of Caribbean Poetry

For readers of West Indian literature, a study of Eric Roach requires no justification. He is the most significant poet in the English-speaking Caribbean between Claude McKay (who spent nearly all of his life abroad) and Derek Walcott. Roach began publishing in the late 1930s and continued, with a few interruptions, until 1974, the year of his suicide. His career thus spans an extraordinary period of Anglophone Caribbean history, from the era of violent strikes that led to the formation of most of the region's political parties, through the process of decolonization, the founding and subsequent failure of the Federation of the West Indies (1958-1962), and the coming of Independence in the 1960s. This book presents a critical analysis of all of Roach's published poetry, but it presents that interpretation as part of a broader study of the relations between his poetic activity, the political events he experienced (especially West Indian Federation, Independence, the Black Power movement, the "February Revolution" of 1970 Trinidad), and the seminal debates about art and culture in which he participated.

By exploring Roach's work within its conditions, this book aims above all to confirm Roach's rightful place among West Indian and metropolitan poets of comparable gifts and accomplishments.

Laurence Breiner is the author of the critically acclaimed *Introduction to West Indian Poetry*.

ISBN 13:9781845230470
UK List Price: £17.99 US$34.95 CAN$43.95

NEW 2007

TRINIDADIAN WRITERS FROM PEEPAL TREE PRESS

James Christopher Aboud
Kevin Baldeosingh
Faustin Charles
Mark De Brito
Brenda Flanagan
Anson Gonzalez
Vishnu Gosine
Cecil Gray
Ismith Khan
Rabindranath Maharaj
Lelawatee Manoo-Rahming
marina ama omowale maxwell
Ian McDonald
Sharlow Mohammed
Lakshmi Persaud
Jennifer Rahim
Raymond Ramcharitar
Eric Merton Roach
Sam Selvon

Peepal Tree Press is celebrated as the home of challenging and inspiring literature from the Caribbean and Black Britain. We publish fiction, poetry, literary criticism, memoirs and historical studies.

www.peepaltreepress.com

Peepal Tree Press, 17 King's Avenue, Leeds LS6 1QS, UK
Tel: +44 (0) 113 2451703
E-mail: contact@peepaltreepress.com